praise for
plenty enough suck to go around

"Dark, funny, generous and jarring—occasionally tragic but never sentimental."
—Paul Tough, author of *Whatever It Takes*

"Wagner writes with honesty and humor."
—Annie Choi, author of *Happy Birthday or Whatever*

"Imagine if Jack Kerouac had lived through the flood and wrote you a long, personal letter from the wreckage."
—Jonathan Goldstein, author of *Ladies and Gentlemen, the Bible!* and host of CBC and PRI's radio show *WireTap*

"I love it. . . . Floods, fires, hoboes, guns, murder, crawfish, gardens, disappointed moms, boyfriend trouble, videogame restorers, and quite a few flat tires—it's all here."
—Pete Jordan, author of *Dishwasher*

"Cheryl Wagner is at home on the death-defying tightrope between wise and wise-ass. Her voice is ironic and plaintive, surefooted and panicky, the combination that provides the thrills and elevates her memoir to a work of art, unsparing of everything, including itself."
—Jack Pendarvis, author of *Awesome*

plenty enough suck to go around

a memoir of floods, fires, parades, and plywood

CHERYL WAGNER

CITADEL PRESS
Kensington Publishing Corp.
www.kensingtonbooks.com

CITADEL PRESS BOOKS are published by

Kensington Publishing Corp.
850 Third Avenue
New York, NY 10022

All Kensington titles, imprints, and distributed lines are available at special quantity discounts for bulk purchases for sales promotions, premiums, fund-raising, educational, or institutional use. Special book excerpts or customized printings can also be created to fit specific needs. For details, write or phone the office of the Kensington special sales manager: Kensington Publishing Corp., 850 Third Avenue, New York, NY 10022, attn: Special Sales Department; phone 1-800-221-2647.

First printing: May 2009

10 9 8 7 6 5 4 3 2

Printed in the United States of America

Library of Congress Control Number: 2008942172

ISBN-13: 978-0-8065-3103-8
ISBN-10: 0-8065-3103-7

*For all the fine examples—Molly Respess Springfield, Helen Hill,
Elizabeth Wagner, and Alice Kennedy*

contents

Prologue   ix

1. Cast Out   1
2. Expedition Pants and Hobnail Milk Glasses   10
3. What the Fuck?   20
4. What the Fuck? Still   26
5. See Ya, Wouldn't Want to Be Ya   40
6. Happy Cheese Town Far, Far Away   62
7. Pit Bull Jesus   75
8. Backyard Glider   85
9. Plenty Enough Suck to Go Around   93
10. Perfectly Simple Solutions   100
11. You Don't Have to Ask, Do You?   108
12. Real Progress   111
13. Ka-Chunk   118
14. Citizen Loser   130
15. A Monster Moonwalking   147
16. In Bloom   155
17. Disaster Season   167
18. Fall Again   169

19. Tumbleset   184
20. Yellow Flowers, Yellow Letter   193
21. Adieu   199
22. The Happy Dutch   202
23. Birth of a Buzzkill   209
24. A Bullet Ant on the Sting Pain Scale   218
25. More About a Neighborhood Than You Ever
    Cared to Know   225

Acknowledgments   241

prologue

That's a great idea! You should really do that! I don't remember ever consciously deciding that *That's a great idea!* was a fine or even sound organizing principle for my life. By the time my boyfriend, Jake, and I were frantically boarding up our back wall and windows to evacuate for Hurricane Katrina, however, that's how I had been living—mostly in New Orleans—since I was seventeen.

Truth be told, I have spent all of my adult life surrounded by people working on what most Americans would consider to be, at best, time-wasting, esoteric projects. Compiling a discography of every known existing recording of wax cylinder minstrel songs? Great! Building a digital urn for yourself on the Internet? Long overdue! Having a tea party with your pet pig as the guest of honor? What can I bring? Do I want to see a short movie about your tween Arkansas cousin's love of Eminem? Who wouldn't? On a quest to wash dishes in all fifty states? Well, move on in!

In my shortish time on this planet, I have gotten out of bed in the morning and tripped over many snoring bands and outfitted my basset hounds as spacemen for numerous French Quarter dog parades. It seems over the years I have become something of a professional enthusiast, which is weird because I'm also kind of cynical and grumpy. Mostly, this just makes me a typical New Orleanian of a sort.

New Orleans exists for many reasons. And over time it has

evolved into the place where Southerners send their laidback people who can't or won't get with the program—their artists, gay relatives, eternal optimists, funny hat wearers, weirdos, and intellectuals. I guess I'm one of the above, and I have a sneaking suspicion that most Southerners do not want me or my friends back in their towns. Many of us are in New Orleans for a reason: to escape the fundamentalist Other South but still get to live near where we're from.

We're mostly seventeen to sixty, a few older or younger. We collect records, books, fine and trash musical instruments, old video games, pieces of wrought iron, and other ephemera. We go out to clubs, backyards, urban bayous, balconies, heavy metal haunted houses, bowling alleys, and street corners to hear bands play. Some of us travel for years and suddenly reappear; some never leave; some try to leave repeatedly and always boomerang back. Some of us secretly feel we're "too smart to be rich" but then whine about our finances later. Others are trustafarians. Still others are bartenders or coffee servers or AV guys. There are teachers and carpenters and librarians and white- or pink-collar administrators of this or that who work forty-plus hours a week but consider this other life, their *That's a great idea!* life, their real lives. The other life is just what they do to put food in their dog's bowl.

Some are fun junkies, plain and simple. Others are great and not-so-great musicians, makers of sublime or total bullshit art, college or post-college radio geeks, Quarter Rats, T-shirt makers, people who go teach English abroad, gay and straight, history buffs, hippies and hipsters and none of the above, poets, electronic hobbyists who build drum machines, Goths and post-Goths and retro-Goths, Francophiles, Japanophiles, music fans of every stripe, potheads, abstainers, crawfish-addicted or vegan, winners and losers, gourmands, experimental filmmakers, brass band and Mardi Gras Indian superfans, Buddhists, poets, guys with beards obsessed with Tibet, bike people, tattoo artists, and folks who just like to sit reading paperbacks on their front porch.

Whenever one of us leaves, another guy or gal inevitably takes our place, some New Orleanian or Louisianan, some not. I'm talking about all the New Orleans people who would probably not call themselves *bohemian* but who nonetheless do not spend their lives clawing tooth and nail to compete! compete! conquer! conquer! and otherwise lock, stock, and barrel the American Dream.

These are people for whom *That's a great idea!* is a much finer way to live than the standard American sour of *Why in the world would anyone want to do a thing like that?*

plenty
enough
suck
to go
around

Chapter 1

cast out

"Hold it tight!" Jake said.

"I'm holding it as tight as I can," I replied.

Jake and I balanced on a two-and-a-half-foot ledge on the second story of our raised house, each balancing an end of a huge half-wet plywood sheet that was heavy as shit. Jake had nails pressed between his lips and a hammer jammed in his back shorts pocket. My neck started to feel like taut rubber bands. I tried not to look over my shoulder and envision my plummet to the ground below. The night before I had done a rare thing: I had watched the local evening news and seen the angry red blob in the Gulf. And so here we were.

"Just try."

"I am trying!" I said, plopping my end down a second.

"Jesus! Tell me when you're going to do that! You're going to kill us."

"Don't talk about it," I said. "Or I'll be too freaked to stand out here."

The shutters on our Mid-City house were not of the High-Velocity-Miami-Dade-Category-5 variety. They were French and louvered and about a hundred years old. Every hurricane season since the scary 1998 Georges evacuation seven years earlier, I had wanted to do something about those shutters, but never had. I liked the way the sun slanted through when I was reading books in bed, and new ones for our entire double-camelback would have cost the amount of a small car. But most of the iron hardware had rusted off and, for this evacuation as for the Hurricane Cindy one the month before, I twisted some pantyhose and a plastic grocery bag to cinch them tight. I wasn't proud of this. The day-of-reckoning aspect of evacuation always made me feel like a loser.

"Come on, pick it up. We still have to pull the other one out from under the house and haul it up here, too."

"Let's just leave it," I said. "It's not going to cover the whole hole."

"We can't leave it. Half the clapboards are off. The wind will blow out the walls. That tarp isn't gonna do jack."

"If the winds are that bad the side windows are going to blow in anyway," I reasoned. Some of those had air conditioners drooping out of them and the rest had no shutters. Not even louvered ones. I pictured the heavy old window units dropping like cartoon anvils through the next-door neighbor's roof.

"Come on," he said.

I gave the plywood another heave. I leaned in closer to the wall and tried to ignore the wood cutting into my fingers. Out of the corner of my eye I could see our two basset hounds, Aunt Clotilde Robichaux and Buster, on the other side of the eight-foot bedroom window. Their two curious noses greased the bottom panes.

Wham! went Jake's hammer. I jumped slightly on the ledge. *Wham! Wham!* Clo started barking.

"We should never have let Tim take out that post," I said.

"It was termite eaten," Jake grumbled around the nails in his mouth.

"Then we shouldn't have hired the other guy."

Our friend Tim the indie rock carpenter had announced that he would not help us on any tasks that were outside and required the forty-foot extension ladder. He had not retired from the Southern band semi-famous for throwing fried chicken for nothing. He was in the midst of learning the pedal steel guitar. He had too much to live for.

So the old-timer carpenter had seemed like a find. The old-timer had laughed at heights. Yes, he brought his bored young nephew with the shiny gold grill and repeatedly attempted to school him on how a nail gun fired. But then he fired the lackadaisical nephew and started afresh. The old-timer's new partner was his elderly wife who wore a neat Jackie-O wig. She came with him to work and made a picnic of it, setting up a transistor radio and a chair. She sat in our backyard under the breezy banana trees listening to the soul station and eating chips from a small bag, occasionally standing to hand an icy Coke up the ladder. I was pretty sure this was nonstandard, but it was also charming—someone's grandmother still so in love that she wanted to sit on a foldout chair and gaze up at her husband all day.

But then the picnic was over. The old-timer and his wife suddenly stopped coming. Tim made a rare altitude exception and scrambled part way up to check the old-timer's work. He pointed out that for a major structural beam of our back wall, the old-timer had used slim finishing nails not much thicker than fishhooks. And so when the storm warning came down, our back wall was not only still open but also in places little more than tacked together.

"We got hustled," I said. "Tim sucks and the old-timer sucks and we suck. This is bullshit."

"Jeez, will you stop talking? I can't concentrate."

Complaining about the predicament took my mind off the lack of railing between me and my twenty-foot bellybuster to the cement patio below. This seemed like exactly one of those situations I had brought on myself by continuing to live in New Orleans. If instead of moving from a small Louisiana town to New Orleans at seventeen I had fled the South like forward-looking modern careerist girls without money are all supposed to, and moved into one of those New York or Metroanywhere cubbyholes off a subway entrance, then I would not be on the back balcony about to fall to my death now. I would be in my little cubbyhole for nine hours until I got on the train to go back home to my other cubbyhole. Bored maybe. Filled with the famous *"inexorable sadness of pencils / neat in their boxes"* and crammed with *"all the misery of manila folders and mucilage"* like in that choking Roethke poem perhaps, yes. But safe!

We nailed and nailed until we were half-assed boarded up. I packed my laptop containing my just-finished novel. Jake had his computer, his bass, and originals of the documentary we had just finished about America and Louisiana's first and oldest developmentally disabled rock band. A few changes of clothes and two basset hounds and two dog beds, and my small car was crammed full.

Rumor was our next-door neighbor used to be a songwriter for Motown. Now he lived behind barbed wire with his wife and two small children. We usually nodded hello and good-bye when we passed in the alley. For some reason, his five-year-old son called Jake "Donkey Donk." Because Jake played music, on occasion they talked Pro Tools plug-ins across the barbed wire that we had been told a "crazy white family" had erected in the sixties. A few nights before, I thought I had seen his little girl twirling modern dances with some other leotard girls on public access TV. He was getting out of his car with some morning doughnuts and we were rushing to leave. We were alarmed by his breezy, breakfast gait.

"Didn't you see the news?" Jake asked.

Our neighbor stopped cold with his doughnuts. "What news?" he said.

The big red blot had looked *bad,* we confided. Bright red like a blob movie and scary. We were afraid. Almost a decade living next door, and we'd never spoken to each other this way. His eyes grew wide.

"I'm gonna turn on that news," he said.

This New Orleans story begins not with the storm. It starts, as many New Orleans stories do, with some bureaucratic bungling. And with Charity Hospital. In 1939, with more than two thousand beds and a gleaming Art Deco façade, the new Charity Hospital in New Orleans was the Superdome of hospitals for Louisiana's poor.

Instead of laboring in bed at the family's strawberry farm on the Hungarian Settlement as she had with her first child, my grandmother decided to climb into the truck with my grandfather and drive to New Orleans. Together they left the dirt roads behind and time-traveled to give birth to my mother in the gleaming new hospital on Tulane Avenue.

But my mother was stubborn and late. For a week my grandparents walked under the trees near a relative's house on Joseph Street trying to coax the baby out. Soon my mother arrived. And there, on her birth certificate, appeared my mother's first New Orleans problem. Whether it was a simple misunderstanding, two Hungarian men struggling to make themselves understood, or classic New Orleans ineptitude, we will never know. But instead of *Elizabeth* after my mother's own mother, the clerk typed *Lizzie*. And so my mom entered the world marked with a Charity Hospital flub that still haunts her at government offices to this day.

By the late fifties, my mother was a young woman who hoped never to pick another strawberry. And so she left the settlement for good and moved in the shotgun house on Joseph Street with her aunt Mary to work. Later she moved into the dorms on Tulane Avenue across from Charity Hospital and donned a starched, white nurse hat. She walked across the street to learn from the nuns at the place that had misspelled her name.

What happened next is a story so old it's almost embarrassing to tell. New Orleans stamped my mother's heart. My mother fell in love with the city. That New Orleans gets in people's blood is one of those clichés that also happens to be true. When a cliché is true, I'm never sure if that makes it not a cliché anymore or if that just makes the cliché all the more sad.

The way people love New Orleans and what they love about it is individual. For poor, rural Louisianans from immigrant families like my mother, New Orleans was an international city that appeared over the horizon once you cleared the familiar, murky hurdle of the swamps and lake. It was the big city Louisiana had to offer. New Orleans had a bustling river port and an airport. People hailed from everywhere. There was a small Chinatown. In the fifties, though an old, old city, New Orleans was also for the deep South a strikingly modern place.

During her childhood, Mom lived on a farm with an outhouse and an outdoor clay oven. As a small girl, she attended the all-night wake of her great-grandmother who was laid out in her own living room. But in New Orleans her Hungarian relatives had long enjoyed modern plumbing and funeral homes.

Mom leapfrogged past where the farms and woods and swamps and outhouses ended and into the city where Fats Domino recorded the country's first rock 'n' roll record. By the mid-sixties, she was married and my father worked briefly for Delta. The two grabbed hands and climbed aboard shiny silver airplanes and flew the country for free. This was around the time on TV that *Star Trek* unveiled its famous transporter used to dismantle people one particle at a time and reconstitute them later. I imagine to a farm girl, New Orleans gave my mom a taste of that. When she stepped onto a jumbo jet on the edge of Lake Pontchartrain and stepped out in New York and San Francisco, it must have been like walking on the moon.

Because she had lived in New Orleans as a young woman,

Mom transmitted some open New Orleans attitudes to her five children when she later took a nursing job halfway between New Orleans and the settlement. When I went to play at a professor's kid's house and came home shocked that I had seen a naked clay lady hugging her knees on the edge of the mom's private bathtub, Mom explained, "Oh, that's nothing. That's art."

When I was a child it was clear that life, real life, happened in New Orleans. At Mardi Gras the men drank at the Friendly House and played cards at the VFW hall on Magazine Street. You could peek in and spy your grandpa and uncles in the curling smoke inside until someone shooed you back to eat stuffed peppers with the other children and ladies. On the street were walking krewes of old men dancing by with gin breath, paying perfect strangers crushed paper flowers for whiskery smooches. Old men with cigars in their mouths juked in broad daylight in the street.

When my father died, my aunt Mary showed Mom how to keep moving. Aunt Mary had lost a child, so she knew. People die for no reason and you keep going. I like to think of these two in the late seventies and early eighties dancing down their front steps for the Krewe of Shut-Ins parade with us kids cheering them on. Old woman in a worn housecoat shaking her rump, showing the young mother how you wriggle free of life's palls.

When I moved to New Orleans in the late eighties, before the Internet, people had to actually leave their bedrooms and even their towns and move somewhere to meet anyone who was remotely like themselves. Some of my first New Orleans friends were small-town Southern gay guys, ex–Southern Baptists who longed to don a cape on Decatur Street, a black punk girl sick of Virginia, and a pothead hard-core drummer whose mother had run the Tallahassee Informed Parents for Drug-Free Youth. New Orleans was the place these Southerners chose when they got old enough to finally be spit out of their mean towns. It was the place you came to start your real life, stop hiding your real self, say your true opinions, wear the jacket you always liked and not have a beer bottle hurled at the back of your head from a pickup truck over it, and still be close enough to drive back home to see if your parents loved you yet. When you got to New Orleans, people said, "Come on over." For many it was a place of comfort in exile. It was not just fun. It was home. And so it was important to us.

By the summer of 2005, how a good honor-roll Catholic daughter winds up happily living in sin and blatantly child-free in her thirties was a question my mother no longer asked herself. New Orleans was the place you sent such daughters in hopes of keeping them close to home. They would be living among relatives and people from home but also strangers and freaks. So it has been and so it will always be. These are the daughters you drive into the city on weekends to do something fun with. You don't know exactly what all they're up to, but you packed them with some common sense and you sent them there so they don't starve or move to New York where you'll never see them again.

Jake was aggravated that we were evacuating. Earlier that summer, a storm that wound up coming nowhere near New Orleans had us jamming the two dog beds into the car and scurrying off to Houston. Our friend Stan had laughed and said, "Y'all evacuated for *that*?" and detailed all the hurricane party exploits we had missed. At such times I think Jake wished he lived with a non-evacuator instead of the early evacuator I had become.

And who could blame him? Evacuating mostly sucked. When evacuations became more frequent in the late nineties, I and many other New Orleanians trying to put a rosy spin on things declared them sudden mini-vacations. But they weren't. Evacuations had taken on a disturbing pattern for us. For every unexpected good thing that happened, there was a counterbalancing bad.

During the evacuation to Houston, we had discovered a secret African and Arab immigrant world nestled in the South that we had never known existed, complete with men in traditional African dress pushing goats on dollies. But it cost me $500 later when I blew out my car air-conditioning running it for the dogs until I could sneak them into our motel. Other people we knew came back either merely brainfogged from too much motel cable or claiming they had eaten some unforgettable something at a cousin's house in Lafayette. Maybe we weren't doing evacuations right.

I wanted to leave early in hopes of getting ahead of the Winn Dixie water and batteries freak-out, the mandatory evacuation grumblings and subsequent "I'm not getting locked in that nasty Dome again!" panic that had been raging since people evacuated there for Hurricane Georges. I wanted to leave before my mother started calling every half hour to nag me about her visions of me drowned in the bottom of the New Orleans bowl. Above all, I wanted to be miles and miles ahead of the one-way traffic projectile vomit that was Contraflow.

In the middle of the night next to me in bed, Jake had put the pillow over his head and grumbled, "You just decide."

I'd made reservations at a cheap, pet-proof motel in Memphis so we could check out the historic Peabody Hotel and their Duckmaster parade. Every morning since the 1940s, a Duckmaster had marched his ducks to John Philip Sousa down an elevator onto a red carpet through the Grand Lobby to an indoor marble fountain. I pictured these ducks with a peacocking drum major like St. Augustine or some other raucous New Orleans high school marching band. I liked amazing animals and our basset hounds were rarely that amazing. One day at the mall when I was a kid, I peered into a fluorescent-lit glass box and played electric tic-tac-toe against a shitting chicken. I made good grades at Holy Ghost School, but I lost every quarter I had to this bird. It had made a lasting impression.

expedition pants and hobnail milk glasses

Somewhere before Mississippi we gave up on Memphis. Jefferson Parish sheriff Harry Lee was blustering on the radio that he had canceled his big birthday blowout. A hefty Chinese-American-Louisianan in an even heftier cowboy hat, Lee was a big Willie Nelson fan and a robust singer. He often took the stage at his annual "Chinese Cajun Cowboy Fais Do Do" fund-raiser to belt out crowd favorites like "To All the Girls I've Loved Before" or "Wind Beneath My Wings." His gigantic plaster bust of himself was probably already down at Hilton Riverside, waiting to be showered with fortune cookies.

The way the storm was sucking the fun out of everybody scared me. If the storm missed us and hit Mississippi, the remnants would probably just blow all the way up to Tennessee and rain on our duck parade.

"Let's just go to Gainesville," Jake said.

Jake's mother was a former cheerleader from Georgia who had recently retired from teaching middle school art in Florida. After decades of grimy clay hands and tempura paint, Brenda was a devotee of both swabbing and order. She met us in the front entryway and stood on her tiptoes, with a towel in one hand, hugging Jake.

"I brought this in case you want to wipe off their feet," she said, pointing at Clo and Buster. "Good to see you."

"They're not dirty," Jake protested, kicking off his own shoes. "They've just been riding in the car."

I slid out of my sandals and put them in the designated shoe lineup. I handed Jake Buster's leash.

"Hold him and I'll do Clo first so she doesn't run," I said.

Clo hated having her feet touched and growled like a motor-cycle whenever you approached them. I got down on my hands and knees to wrestle her with Brenda's towel. For an arthritic skeleton, Clo was strong.

Jake's stepfather crunched into the dog-decontamination chamber. Jack was an entomologist with a big white mustache who specialized in the sex lives of fruit flies. He was the only person I'd ever met who had a parasitoid that eats flies named after him.

"How was your trip?" Jack said.

"Ah, you know," Jake shrugged.

"It's a long booger," Jack agreed, bending down to pet Buster. "Buster, how you doing, old boy? Looking regal as ever. Play your cards right and we'll be going to TCBY."

In his post-divorce days before he met Jake's mom, Jack had lived wild and free with his two children, a cocker spaniel named Rex, and a free-roaming gecko on patrol for natural pest control. Now his two children were young adults. He was down to only an extensive collection of dead bugs on pins and Brenda's obese and dying cat, Oreo. Dog-lonesome, he showered Buster and Clo with vanilla frozen yogurts and six-dollar dental bones whenever they visited.

"Did you move the potatoes?" I asked Jake's mom.

"I remembered the potatoes, but Jack, I think you forgot the puffer fish," Brenda said.

Clo's paws were as antiseptic as they were going to be. I got up and handed off the towel to Jake to swab Buster. "I'll move it," I said.

No matter how long it was between visits, Buster and Clo remembered their favorite trouble spots. Buster would beeline for the bowl of potatoes on a cart in the kitchen. Clo favored the hairy, Southwestern fertility tchotckes and animal bones on display on some tables and low shelves. When they weren't locked in the garage, the two would go around smearing their wet noses on things and Brenda would scramble to decontaminate the spots. I decided to attempt to keep at least Clo on her leash for the entire visit.

Jack stretched flat out on his back on the living room floor next to Buster.

"I don't know why, but Buster reminds me of Winston Churchill," Jack said.

Buster raised his chin slightly for Jack to scratch his soft throat. Still on her leash, Clo flattened herself next to my feet and grumbled, pouting.

"It's all that skin on his neck," I said. "It's like an ascot."

"You know you might be right. I always chalked it up to his bone structure," Jack said. "I was reading this article about truffle pigs the other day and I thought, Buster could do that. Before you leave, Jake and Buster and I might need to go out Chicken-of-the-Woods mushroom hunting."

Brenda wandered into the kitchen.

"Jake," Brenda called over the counter. "What do you think you might feel like eating for supper? I could make spaghetti. You like that."

"I'm not really that hungry," Jake said. "But thanks."

Jake's mother was always saying some dish was his favorite and Jake was always saying the opposite behind her back, that some dish was so leaden with onions that it left him doubled over, clutching his stomach. This had been going on for at least the entire nine years that Jake and I had been together. I did not know why and I did not care to know why. We should have gone to Memphis. I wondered what those marching Peabody Hotel ducks were doing. Probably wearing hats, cruising that gilded travertine pond.

"I'm calling my mom to see if she's going to evacuate," I told Jake.

"I wonder if Flash left," Jake said. "I wonder if Stan left."

"Hopefully," I said.

Mom's a Super Doppler 6000 fan and possibly an addict. Sometimes when I'm on my way to visit her or she's on her way to visit me, she'll call at the last minute and reschedule.

"There's a supercell over Manchac," she'll say. "You better wait."

Jake got her a weather radio for Christmas. A few years before that we got her a spooky balsa wood Indian weather stick. You nail it to a tree or wall and it bends up for sunny weather and down for rain. When I was a teenager, I found her weather obsession maddening. Later, I attributed it to her friend's husband who got killed in Mississippi trying to save his boat from Hurricane Camille. Lately, I wondered if it was from being a child on a farm in the forties, watching her father look up at a darkening sky and wonder if they were going to have any money that year.

"Are they evacuating Hammond or not?" I asked.

"Only up to the interstate where it's low-lying," she said. "Where we are it's optional."

"So they're mandatory evacuating within a few miles from you, but you're not going to leave," I said. "Why don't you just go to Baton Rouge?"

I had heard that a lot of people in Mom's area were driving up to Baton Rouge to try to get out of the reach of the worst of the looming storm. We have family there, so I knew Mom and my developmentally disabled sister Lori who lived with her would have a place to stay.

"I don't want to get stuck on that interstate," Mom said. "We're not going to flood here."

"Probably not," I said. "But why every time there's a big thunderstorm do you call me to complain that a pine or an oak tree is going to fall on your house?"

"Because one did! Twice! I have two other trees I need to get checked. But those men want a thousand dollars!"

"If it's going to fall on your house in a bad thunderstorm, why don't you think it's going to fall on your house now? It might be a Category five, Mom. Why don't y'all at least drive up the street to the arena? Did they open it?"

"Yes," she admitted. "But I don't want Lori to have to get stuck in all that traffic or get stuck all night in the arena."

"Lori might enjoy it. It'll be a commotion," I said.

In Hammond, Lori walked around like she was the Strawberry Queen. New caregivers were always surprised how many people knew Lori. Thick, country black ladies and thin, white Pentecostal women would call out to Lori across the movie theater parking lot to greet her with her own sayings. "Hey sweetheart, you get that money?" they'd say. Lori would holler back, "Yeah, swee-heart, two dolluhs!"

"*Maybe* she'd like it," Mom said. "For half an hour. But when she's ready to go, you better believe she's ready to go. Then what?"

"Bring a Valium," I suggested.

"Sure," she said. "No thanks."

When I was growing up, I was in charge of Lori, and it is understood that one day I will be again. In recent years, I do very little besides get weekly debriefings, like at any moment the Cheryl-Jake regiment could be called to active duty. Consequently, I usually know whether Lori and her sheltered workshop

co-workers are packing bay leaves or shredding hospital docu-
ments and which developmentally disabled person in her small
town called which other developmentally disabled person a bitch
that week. Although Mom still worked and did not act elderly,
she had gotten her Medicare card awhile back and cruised in a
boat-sized Mercury Grand Marquis. Sometimes I worried that
any day I might have to step in and pry Lori from her suddenly
demented fingers.

"If your trees are rotten, they're rotten," I said.

"If we need to go at the last minute, we will," she said.

This seemed like a lie, and a weird one.

"You know the winds come first. Then you'll be stuck."

"Tell Jake his radio is working good. We'll just pull the mattresses and sleep in the hallway like we used to for a tornado
warning," she said. "Lori likes the hallway."

"That's a terrible idea," I told Mom.

Brenda glanced up wide-eyed from her cutting board. I took
the phone outside so Jake's family would not overhear any more
foolishness. I wasn't sure Florida people had to talk to their relatives like this to get them to evacuate.

"I want you to really think about this. I don't think Lori can
handle being in some six-hour storm with stuff crashing on the
house. She'll be scared."

Silence. I couldn't believe it. Mom was hyper-responsible. To
her own detriment usually. Not in my wildest dreams did I think
it would have been necessary to swing by their house on our way
out of town to snatch Lori.

"If you make a bad decision for yourself that's one thing, but I
don't think it's fair to Lori," I said. "You're in charge. It's not like
she gets a choice."

"You think I don't know that?" she said.

"Well, you're making me stressed."

"Stop worrying. Go enjoy your visit. We'll be fine."

I stepped back inside. Clo was in the foyer waiting. Jake and Buster were sitting on the back of their necks watching *Murder She Wrote*. I knelt down on the floor to hug Clo.

"She won't evacuate," I said to Jake.

Jake sat up. "What?" he asked. "With all she bugs us about the tiniest weather crap? That's crazy. Tell her to go to Baton Rouge. She's going to wind up there anyway when her power goes out for a week."

"Don't tell *me*. She could just go up the street and she won't. She said she's going to lay on a mattress in the hallway with Lori and your radio," I said. "We should have never given her that radio."

Jake shook his head and laughed.

"It's not funny," I said. "What if something happens?"

"I know it's not funny," Jake said. "I don't think it is. I just keep picturing them on that mattress."

"I'm really worried."

Jack strode into the living room wearing his expedition pants. Its safari pockets were bulging. He smiled.

"Who wants to go mushroom hunting?"

Jake's aunt had left some hobnail milk glass dishes and *Gone with the Wind* lamps in Florida for me. I e-mailed to thank her and she e-mailed back.

> I'm glad y'all are safe and sound. Hope the house is almost finished so you can quit spending all your time painting. It would be terrible if something happened to your house, but it also might be a good thing. You could rebuild with insurance and everything would be new!

It would be more than a pain. We would have nowhere to live. The whole people getting an MTV-style crib after a fire or mud-slide or disaster seemed pure urban legend—perhaps one people retold to make themselves feel better about emptying their pockets to insurance companies. Injury was injury. I had never met a single person who emerged from a car accident or a house fire fundamentally better off than they were before they went in. I didn't believe in clouds with silver linings. I believed in clouds.

After the mushroom hunt, Jake sprawled back out on the living room floor, lost in cable TV, his preferred retreat position when visiting home. I looked up from my laptop.

"Deanna thinks if we lose our house we'll be blinging in a McMansion," I said.

He grimaced and shook his head. "I don't want to talk about it."

We were no financial analysts. In the nineties when our landlord wanted to dump our house because it needed a new roof, gutter, and porches and he was sick of paying old men $10 to nail flattened tin over broken windows and floors, we jumped on it. Jake had signed on the dotted line when he was twenty-four so he, I, his drummer, and an artist friend could all keep cheap rent. For some reason, the fact that we both worked and jammed the rest of our time with music and writing projects and had no carpentry skills or repair money between us was no deterrent.

Jake's drummer at the time was a Memphis art school dropout from Arkansas who waited tables at Commander's Palace. Even though we had all hung out the upstairs windows slapping on the first coat of primer that had touched the house in decades, we barely passed inspection. Our initial inspector, a woman who had just passed her inspector test, took one look at the house and shook her head. She told us she did not want to lose her new license. The inspector slid us the number of a portly Yes Man who arrived mouthing a cigar. This ancient Yes Man doddered around the property, declining to huff upstairs or bend down to peek under our raised house at all. He told Jake how he had strafed German trains in World War II. He thought Jake looked like a nice young man who would have enjoyed it. We passed with flying colors.

During the evacuation before this evacuation, Jake and I had talked about pulling our heads out of the clouds and getting our shit together. We were overexposed in more ways than one. Our house had appreciated in value since the bargain-basement nineties, and we were underinsured. But after we got back from that evacuation, our vow to set our house of cards in order somehow got lost in our whirl of whirl.

My mom, who saw us most often, had long lamented that our entire management system was more a case study than a best-practices text. She would give me flowered file folder boxes for gifts. Picking her way through amps, guitars, cords, piles of books, recently stripped shutters, and a friend's oversized paintings of outer space on her way to the bathroom, she would announce, "Someone is going to break their neck!"

The weather forecasters were really enjoying themselves. They were shaking their arms at the digital red blob like it was the latest dance.

"I'm going to bed," Jake announced. "I'm not watching this all night to see if it turns or not."

I was exhausted but needed to stay up to see if the storm was going to veer far enough toward Mississippi to miss us. This guilty last-minute wishing is the dirty secret of the final hours of storm watching—thousands of Louisianans and Mississippians pitted against one another wherever they are, screaming into their televisions at the wobbling red curse on the satellite, *Go left!* or *Go right!*

Sometime in the wee hours my mother's electricity went out. I called her and her voice sounded thin. The wind was howling and now she wanted to go to the shelter. It was too late. She sounded frightened and old.

"What's the Weather Channel say?" she asked.

The TV kept saying it was the widest storm ever. It said it would go on for a deliciously long time. The TV was excited. It could not wait for us to get hit. I didn't have the heart to tell her what was coming her way was hours and hours from ending. Her health had not been great in the past few years. I felt sick. I hoped she did not have a heart attack listening to the wind howl and waiting for her trees to fall. I slunk off to bed.

When I woke up a few hours later, I called Mom back. Her cell phone was out. I called her on her house phone. It was out, too. I turned on the television. There was no point willing it this way or that. It was too big. Jake's mother padded into the kitchen.

"How's it going?" she said.

"Terrible," I replied. "My mom's phone went out."

Chapter 3

what the fuck?

From: Cheryl
To: Everybody
Subject: It takes awhile to open but it has a satellite pic of n.o.
taken Wednesday

You can see where the water starts and stops by block at least
if you trace it back from landmark streets etc. When the street is
dark, it's b/c it's filled with water seems like

cheryl

From: Cheryl
To: Fontenot
Subject: Re: how are things?

I hope j. did not hole up w/ his parents in n.o. east. The stuff
online at wwl is terrible. we thought we were okay but now we're
worried our house flooded in that levee break b/c they said the
flooding got as far as mid-city. They're not letting us back yet,
so only time will tell . . . my mom's trees fell on her neighbor's
house in hammond but she is okay but no electricity . . . i hope
we don't wind up in some kind of mad max situation guarding our
wreckage!

cheryl

From: Stoo
To: Cheryl
Subject: Fwd: Katrina hopes & fears

Here ya go . . . Remember this is a couple days old. There is a
map floating around in Yahoo News Photos of where the flooding
is. Irish Channel looks virtually unscathed. Mid-City looks fucked
up, alas. Rumor is they're evacuating my parents from Touro
Hospital as we speak. No one knows to where.

Kisses, odom

From: Helen
To: Cheryl
Subject: we're okay

Cheryl!
I'm so glad to hear from you. I assume Jake's okay too. We
are certainly in the same boat with our Mid-City homes. Paul
and Francis and I and Rosie the pig are safe at my parents'
in Columbia, SC. I heard that the Jesuit high school had 9 feet
of water inside. I miraculously got in touch by cellphone with a
neighbor, Derrlyn, who stayed behind because she is a cop
in training. She was optimistic that our street wasn't flooded
too badly, but that was Tuesday morning. She hadn't been able
to get back to Mid-City. I figure our houses are pretty flooded,
if standing. Paul will go back to investigate when he feels it is
safe, and may be allowed back earlier since he is a doctor at a
state hospital. I know Rene is fine and has kept his sense of
humor, emailing me that the 8 ball outlook of my film class
show at Zeitgeist on Oct. 2 is not so good.

love from Helen

From: Alex
To: Cheryl
Subject: Re: It takes awhile to open but it has a satellite pic of
n.o. taken Wednesday

thank you so much! my house may not be flooded as much as
I thought or even at all. I can see some green spots around my
neighborhood. makes sense because we're above sea level
unlike the rest of Lakeview which is totally submerged. I hope
that's the case . . .

Alex

From: Fontenot
To: Cheryl
Subject: Re: how are things?

Any word about J. and his family? This whole thing is horrific
and unbelievable. I've been angry and frustrated for the last
two days. How are you doing?

From: Cheryl
To: Fontenot
Subject: Re: how are things?

the rage is about to kill me. i am so angry. we're getting more
and more news of friends who had to walk out of the city and
HITCHHIKE to Lafayette, others still stuck, friends parents
with cancer left on hospital rooftops and airlifted out just this
morning. not to mention the HORROR of not dropping any water
for all those old people and not getting them out. disgusting and
criminal.

mom and lori went on to baton rouge because no electricity.
i'm emailing and calling around and trying to see where j. might
be. i assume he left n.o. east with his parents?

From: Fontenot
To: Cheryl
Subject: Re: how are things?

I feel the exact same way. This morning I walked out of my apartment feeling like I wanted to start punching the wall. Let me know if you get any news about J.

From: Jake and Cheryl
To: Helen
Subject: Fwd: makes me cry-photos from mid-city landmarks

Here are some photos from mid-city that someone just sent me.

Cheryl and Jake

From: Bobbie
To: Cheryl
Subject: Red Cross will give you a debit card

hey,

it is true. we went to red cross tuesday and they gave our household $965. my mom got $360 for her self. the catch . . . you only have 15 days to spend it!

anyway, i just read an e-mail from my friend who is stuck in new orleans and who is also a police officer. she said it really is as bad there as the national news makes it out to be. we should truly stay away until they say it is safe to return. she said people were insane. they were stealing stuff just for the sake of stealing it. they broke into blockbuster and stole dvds. oh the horror!!!!!! our house is totally completey ruined. it makes me sick.

talk to you later.

Bobbie

From: Cheryl
To: Jim
Subject: Re: news?

how long do you think house wiring can sit submerged in water before it corrodes, rots, or is otherwise unusable in yr professional estimation? that is if the foundation does not collapse?

From: Jim
To: Cheryl
Subject: Re: news?

I have no idea about the wiring. If the water is salty, I don't know. Maybe you get some FEMA money and rewire the place completely. Put a whole new service in. That'd be best, wouldn't it?

Came across our pictures of you and Jake on your steps yesterday. What's your address there?

From: Cheryl
To: Helen
Subject:?

dear helen,

hope y'all are all still doing well over there. I'm wanting all my hammering back that i did at my dumb, soaked house since april (and 1998)!

Cheryl

From: Fontenot
To: Cheryl
Subject: the lucky poor

Barbara Bush: Things Working Out 'Very Well' for Poor
Evacuees from New Orleans By E&P Staff

In a segment at the top of the show on the surge of evacuees to
the Texas city, Barbara Bush said: "Almost everyone I've talked
to says we're going to move to Houston."

Then she added: "What I'm hearing which is sort of scary is they
all want to stay in Texas. Everyone is so overwhelmed by the
hospitality.

"And so many of the people in the arena here, you know, were
underprivileged anyway, so this—this (she chuckles slightly)
is working very well for them."

From: Mom
To: Cheryl
Subject: Re: Fwd: Hurricane Katrina—Our Experiences

that just makes me so sick. It's hard to believe, but i know it's
true. i hear only sadness.

love, mom

what the fuck? still

It seemed suspicious to some of Tanio's friends that he had refused invitations to Burning Man for well over a decade. He used to play in Berkeley-area dissonance-funk bands and frequent Barrington Hall punk "Wine Dinners." He used to sculpt metal. He had friends with both trampolines and half-pipes in their converted-storefront living rooms. He worked at a video-game company with a friend who had a trapdoor that led to an arcade game museum under his kitchen. All this made it suspect that Tanio had never cared to see the desert art spectacle that was Burning Man. Tanio tried to explain that he liked to shower and hated being sandy. He had not been raised to show his genitals in the desert.

Nonetheless, they had finally gotten to him. A woman who used to work with KoKo the gorilla was setting everything up. Bike, tent, food, goggles. All he had to do was show up on August 30.

But Tanio was a Nola expat. His stepmother's business had just flooded on Napoleon Avenue. The hurricane just washed away his dad's retirement plan—smashing his fishing camp in Pass Christian and punching holes in his sailboat. With New Orleans underwater and martial law, his family was stuck off in a hotel somewhere. And his co-dog, Clotilde Robichaux, was flooded and homeless. It all made for one big Burning Man bummer.

Tanio and I had seen each other through the green part of our twenties. Some people thought it was odd that we were still friends. I preferred to think of us like one of those old, gay ex-couples who still strapped on a few sequins or chaps and buddied around for Decadence in the Quarter every few years— especially when the other paradigm seemed to be all my friends' bitter, incommunicado divorced parents.

"This is the guy I'm going to hang out with," Tanio e-mailed.

Attached was a news photo of a bespectacled, twenty-seven-year old antisocial who planned to seal himself inside a ten-by-ten Plexiglas box to observe Burning Man's tripping art festers from a close but insulated distance.

"Can you believe this shit is going on and Tanio is hanging out with the boy in the plastic bubble?" I asked Jake.

"Yes," Jake said. "I mean, no. I don't know. He better figure out where his dog is going to live."

"Clo's mine," I reminded him.

Clo didn't look homeless. She looked plenty relaxed stretched across her foam bed by the fireplace. She peered out of two slits when she heard her name, but decided not to get up.

"She's not yours if he took her and then tried to give her back. She's his," Jake pointed out. "Especially if we don't have anywhere to live."

A few years prior, Tanio had given Clo back to me, and I had accepted her on the semi-down-low. My subterfuge had gotten on Jake's nerves. But I felt bad for Tanio. He loved Clo. His neighbor, a ghostly thin medical marijuana devotee trailing an IV pole, had confronted Tanio in his Oakland driveway one night, claiming that Clo's barking was literally killing him. In Clo's hour of need, I had shocked both Buster and Jake by welcoming my first dog back with greedy, open arms. Irritated, Jake warned that Clo was sent back South because she was now an ornery grandmother—one that would ultimately require intensive hospicing.

I had told Tanio there was nothing he could do to help New Orleans or his family all the way from California, but I was starting to wonder. Cavorting at Burning Man when your family and co-dog's future was in serious question seemed sketchy.

"You know y'all could come out here if you need to," Tanio had told me on the phone. "I can send money if you need it. I can leave you a key."

"I know," I said. "We really appreciate it."

"Only I'm not sure what we'd do about Clo and Buster. In my new building they won't let me have them."

The next ten days hurt. All the LSU hurricane doomsday guy's dire prognostications were coming true. Fire, floods, floods on fire. The giant ball of floating ants arrived. Our governor and mayor were on the television with eyes red from crying.

The phone kept ringing and what was coming out of it hurt my ears. Friends stuck on balconies and roofs, friends calling crying because they thought they killed their cats, a woman dead on the sidewalk on my friend's block, a friend handed a rifle and commanded to guard kids on respirators, rumors of friend's parent's neighbors dangling from trees in Mississippi. No one had ever called me to say things like that, much less so many people.

We didn't know what to do. Our friends didn't know what to do. No one knew what to do. As days passed, it seemed the single worst idea was to make irrevocable life decisions based on the crazy TV. Television reporters held microphones up to New Orleanians who screamed things like, "These old people are needing water! Get us the hell out of here!" and the reporters, well-coiffed and hydrated, had turned back to the camera and opined, "It's hard to say what would help this situation that has so gravely deteriorated here. . . . " People were suffering, not speaking a foreign language.

"THEY SAID THEY NEED WATER AND TO GET OUT OF THERE," I yelled at the TV before Jake would turn it off.

Feeling guilty, well-fed, and helpless, I camped out on the bed with my laptop and cell phone. I tried to help friends find lost people. I transferred the desperate Please-Go-Save-My-Elderly-Aunt-and-Disabled-Cousin-Stuck-on-Palmyra-Street postings of strangers from nola.com into the correct Coast Guard rescue website and then called their emergency phone number and repeated it. It seemed inconceivable that this could help, yet also inconceivable that people were posting desperate SOSs on the Web that trapped relatives had phoned to them in the first place. Jake walked back to the bedroom occasionally. "Are you still doing that?" he said. "Fuck!" he exhaled, falling face-first next to me on the bed.

Our two-night evacuation jaunt had long since turned to Jake's worst trip home ever. Something about wiping the dogs by-now sterile feet five times a day and padding around barefoot for no reason to protect hardwood flooring only emphasized the river of water on our own street. The longer we were there, the edgier Jake got around his mother. A few days into the long-distance mayhem, into spectating our own disaster, Jake stopped shucking his shoes every time he walked in the door.

One day we were getting out of the house, driving with both dogs hanging out opposite back windows on one of those nowhere drives around Gainesville, just taking in all the orange-and-blue bunting on squat cement buildings for University of Florida's upcoming first game of the season. Maybe I was trying some time-worn coping strategies on for size—wrapping a lot of words around the spreading wound—because I was prattling on that in the great scheme of things, in the *cosmos* scheme of things, how insignificant we all were, how our existence was fleeting galaxy confetti and, as such, it didn't matter. Losses or gains, all the same. Jake looked at me like he wished I would shut up.

"You know that was everything we've been working for," Jake said.

He was right. I felt it in my chest. Galaxy confetti or not, we had to trod this earthly veil—if we weren't lucky, as two full-grown adults on someone's mom's couch or under a bridge. Shit.

Since Jack and Brenda had recently both sero-converted to birding, the backyard had sprouted contraptions stocked with peanut butter, carob, nuts, and granola. The view out the back patio doors was a study of bird and squirrel obesity. During visits I would sit on the sofa with a book or laptop open, and, if Clo was acting too crazy trotting from garbage can to garbage can, her leash in my hand. Jake was slumped in a soft chair near me watching some rare Florida woodpeckers gorge themselves extinct, when his mom brought up some retention pond across town for the third time that day.

"Do you think we could flood here? Maybe we should check our insurance," she fretted.

"No," Jack said. "Not at all."

"The rainwater hit the edge of the patio that time," Brenda said.

Jack frowned and shook his head.

"It did," Brenda insisted.

"That is miles away," he said.

Jake had settled into a look of stony misery by then, yet it seemed this flood fantasy might either crumble him completely or snap him to scary life. I reached over and squeezed his hand. I wondered if people across America were sitting watching the black water rise and seeing water stains blotting their own curtains and floors. It was either the sickest form of empathy ever or the most pure. I couldn't tell which.

As days wore on, everyone's short-term evacuation plans unraveled. Friends called to say they were running out of motel money but had nowhere else to go. People started sounding weird. A lawyer friend said he had gone and bought all new clothes at Wal-Mart and he was going to relax and go to northern California for a while, probably quit lawyering all together. Get a job sweeping up at a Starbucks or something. O-kaaay, I said.

"I'm going for a walk," I told Jake.

I was taking the dogs on long rambles a few times a day to try to clear my head. Around the subdivision into a nearby school's sandy back lot and around again we'd go, rickety Clo trotting ahead and sometimes falling to her arthritic knees. Buster and I hustled to keep up. My cell phone rang. I answered and held it a little away from my ear. The heat of people's news was giving me an automatic headache.

"Aunt Mary's son won't leave Uptown and he's too old. He doesn't have enough water. People are acting crazy. His kids are worried sick."

I didn't know what to say. She did the same thing, only not in the worst place. It made me wonder about that infamous Hungarian (or was it Louisianan?) stubbornness.

"And I have some sad news. You know my cousin Dorothy we go take berries to?"

When Dorothy was a city teenager and Mom was a little settlement girl, Dorothy would come visiting from New Orleans. Mom was Dorothy's favorite. Dorothy used to sneak Mom to the outhouse and smoke a cigarette, then threaten to stick my mom's head down the black hole if she told. More recently, she was sick. Mom and I would go to her little house in Metairie during spring with a flat of Albany strawberries. Mom would say, "These are the sweet ones, not like they're planting now," and Dorothy would tear up over her oxygen mask. The ghosts of city cousin and country cousin would rise in the sickroom between us—two girls in hand-sewn cotton dresses, grappling in an outhouse over a cigarette in the forties.

"What about Dorothy? Is she okay?"

"Well, your cousin who takes care of her? He died in Houston during the evacuation. In his motel."

"What?" I said.

"They had to put Dorothy in the ICU, and he saw on TV about the hospitals losing power and thought his mom died. He felt guilty for leaving her there. He shot himself. But Dorothy made it fine."

I stopped walking.

"What the fuck. If anybody was doing his damn job, this wouldn't be going on so long," I said. "People's minds are breaking."

Mom was silent.

"I'm sorry I'm cursing. I can't help it. I need to do something."

"There's nothing you can do. You have enough to worry about. I just thought you'd want to know. I have to go. Roberta's coming in a minute to drop off stuff. I'm washing state trooper underwear."

"Why are you washing state trooper underwear?" I asked, feeling a million pointless miles away.

"They need me to. Other people are going to hand out toothbrushes for the Red Cross."

"We're going in as soon as the water goes down. Maybe sooner."

"How are you going to get in?" Mom said. "Just stay put where you are. There's nothing you can do."

"Did Harvey and them go over there with their fan boats?" I asked.

"I haven't heard if they did or not," she said. "I wouldn't be surprised."

I had read online that Cajun and fishermen types had heard the call and were chugging into the city with their outboard motors and fan boats to help. I pictured my father's best friend, a Cajun alligator and turtle farmer and swamp man whom I'd always liked but, as a child, been vaguely afraid of, steaming over from Lake Maurepas down my street to rescue left-behind neighbors. It was surreal to think of my whole known universe folding up on itself like that. Like Raid Man—the bald man who lived alone with ten cans of Raid lined up near his front door for macing kids who walked too close to his porch. I pictured Raid Man stranded and lonesome on his roof, his cans of Raid bobbing down the street. Would Raid Man take the hand of Swamp Man and step into his boat?

"Just stay put," Mom said. "I think Roberta's here. I have to go."

The dogs and I strolled around the corner. Near the cracked and empty racquetball court that shielded the neighborhood from the cars whizzing by, Buster peed on the grass. Not to be outdone, Clo squatted and let loose a stream on top. Across the street, an old, pale man with slicked-back gray hair and suspenders came rushing out of his house. The day before, Jake and I had walked by a house and been amazed to see a small bag of dog poop hanging in effigy from a nasty sign in the middle of a lawn. What kind of people hung dog poop in effigy? "Florida people," Jake had said.

"We have a real problem around here with dog waste," the old man yelled. "Real big problems."

I took a deep breath. I looked at the square lawns lined up in a rigid row. Forever in a drought and loosening their belts only on game day, the stucco-over-cinderblock houses full of mean, mean north Florida people. I could not wait to get back home to New Orleans. The old man stepped off his curb toward us and blocked the street. An aging country bully and sadsack us—his last viable targets.

"We don't live here and I pick hers up anyway," I said, waving my empty white plastic bag like a flag. "She just peed."

"That's what I'm saying. Urination! All dog waste!"

In New Orleans, you could walk your dog for miles without getting yelled at. In New Orleans, strangers would roll down their car windows and tell you about the first basset they had and how his feet smelled like popcorn. Old men would stop their bicycles, tip their hat, and pet your dog. In New Orleans, people who knew how to live were dying and in Florida the life misers and sapsuckers of this world dragged on and on.

"How can I pick up pee?" I yelled. "Get a real problem!"

I was surprised to see the old man backing up and going into his house. Maybe I seemed unhinged. I was embarrassed. I had never before wanted to punch an old man in the face.

"I yelled at your neighbor," I confessed to Jack when I walked in the door. "I'm very sorry, but he really deserved it."

The edges of Jack's white mustache sagged. He had already set up a scrubby, shade-friendly native plant habitat under the towering trees in his yard instead of clear-cutting and rolling out a neat lawn carpet. He had told his neighbors that this was because he was an entomologist, but he was probably mounting a one-man restoration of Florida's hardwood hammock habitat. Now he had gone and introduced two bassets and New Orleanians to the mix, upsetting the delicate neighborhood ecosystem.

"Which neighbor?" he said.

"On the corner. Maybe you shouldn't walk in that direction anymore."

"Which corner?"

"By the highway," I said. "The old dog poop nazi. In suspenders."

"Okay then," Jack said. "Well. I never liked that direction anyway."

Sometime after the frat guys started to line their kegs up along Main Street and break out their jumbo blue-and-orange foam fingers and their perma-tanned girlfriends started to back-that-ass-up behind them, we went to stand in the Red Cross line with the other victims. We had our dogs, our laptops, one car, a weekend's worth of clothes, a flooded house, and, being freelancers, no idea when we would have work again. We had bills due and savings I was hoping not to touch unless absolutely necessary.

I don't know when the white envelopes started arriving, but they were worse than the Red Cross line. Family friends started giving us envelopes with money like at a Southern funeral. Someone is in big trouble, I thought, seeing the handwritten checks for $20 or $30. Something about the white envelopes made our totally-fuckedness seem more official. The first envelope Brenda pressed into my hand, I did not want to take.

Because the house was small and walls were thin and Jake was tired of seeing his mom crying, we were whispering a lot by then.

"Hey," I whispered to Jake in bed one night, pointing to the small but growing pile of envelopes on the nightstand. "They must think we're really bad off. We're not *that* bad off."

"How do you figure?" he asked.

It was not that I thought the whole flooded house and flooded van and dubious employment outlook of dead city thing was just a mild setback, it was that I knew other people were worse off. True, we might have to start over from scratch somewhere we didn't want to be with next to nothing, but we had college degrees with which to hopefully quickly get emergency jobs we hated.

"We're not dead," I said. "We're not on a roof or in a shelter. We have a car left. We evacuated and didn't have to swim to the interstate and heatstroke in the sun and see firsthand the shit that is going to ruin people's lives."

At moments the TV and the WWL Internet radio blow-by-blow rendered our real disaster virtual and creepy, an electronic porthole with a very real sea whipping on the other side of the glass.

What you saw out that window might rob you of something. But the glass also buffered you from it.

"We don't have anywhere to *live*. We can't stay here. We can't go to your mom's. We don't have any clothes. I lost all my equipment. We're down to one crappy car."

"I can't help it," I said. "I feel like we should give at least some of those envelopes to someone else."

Jake looked at me like I was crazy.

"We're keeping them," Jake said. "Do you have any clue what this is going to cost? What this has already cost? We're taking everything and anything we can get."

In the turbulent fifties and sixties in north Florida, Jake's grandfather was a well-loved, anti-segregationist Methodist minister. One day a white envelope came in the mail addressed in shaky old cursive to Jake. "You don't know me," the note inside said. "But your grandfather saved my life."

"That's crazy. That's crazy," Jake said. "Are you serious? That's crazy. I don't know, man. I don't know."

"What?" I said. "What?"

Jake shushed me. "I don't know about that, man. Well, yeah . . . maybe. I hope not. I don't know. So you say. I don't know. Be careful."

"What?"

Jake made a gun with his hand and cocked his thumb.

Dave kept calling and talking about guns and mean dogs, which was strange. Dave used to play occasional percussion in Jake's band and, in his own band, sang sweet falsetto Cuban songs of love. He lived a block away in Mid-City and was getting together his own Rush cover band. He was a very convincing Geddy Lee. What did he need with a gun?

He and his new wife, Marcelle, had evacuated to her parents in Baton Rouge. The television news was whipping people up and now Baton Rougers were spreading rumors that people from New Orleans were raping and looting their mall. Dave was saying he was going back to his wreckage with a gun and some mean dogs.

"No one's raping anyone at the mall in Baton Rouge," I said.

Unlike people whose every family member and friend lived in the greater New Orleans or the Mississippi Gulf Coast area, we were not without short-term options. A music video director friend called to say he wanted, no *needed*, some hip Katrina refugees to accessorize his couch out in L.A. Old roommates materialized from the ether e-mailing that they could keep one or the other of us for a few weeks. But what about after a few weeks, and what about Buster and Clo? People kept saying there was no New Orleans and there wouldn't be for at least a month until they pumped the water out and then what was left would be dregs. How could a city be dregs? It did not seem possible. I refused to believe it.

Jake and Paul kept puzzling about insurance on the phone. Paul and Helen were friends of ours in Mid-City. Paul was from Canada and Helen was a filmmaker from South Carolina I had met in the late nineties at a film festival in Charleston. She had shown a charming, handmade film about her grandfather who could do handstands and where loved people go when they die. She told me she used to live in New Orleans and was moving back and would look me up when she returned, and she did. Later Jake and Helen taught a video class together for teens. They and the kids made a stop-motion animation of squirrels that smoked cigarettes and fell from their tree.

Jake and Paul both were in bands. We were similar, but different. Paul and Helen were cheery freebirds who dressed colorfully and as they pleased. The jobs I'd had required me *not* to wear most of the clothes I wore the rest of the time. We were just vegetarians; they were vegans. We had chubby Buster; they

had Rosie, a miniature pig who loved cookies and had swelled
to a snorting, barnyard size that Buster feared. My backyard
chickens-and-compost-phase lasted only a few months until my
neighbors complained about the crowing. They invited their
neighbors over for cotton candy parties. I usually avoided mine.

But once Paul and Helen bought a house in Mid-City, they always had an open door. My mom and I sometimes strolled over to
Helen's while Paul was at work to see what was germinating on
her cluttered animation table or admire her towering sunflowers
or trial lettuce patch. Strolling to Helen's house with my mom
reminded me of Saturday drives we took to the settlement when
I was a kid to see what vegetables or berries or pecans relatives
had ripening.

A radio show I had done work for previously called, and I did
a flood story that I was surprised my fingers could still type. I
knew Helen liked the show and was marooned, too, so I told her
to listen. She e-mailed back.

Just now I heard your piece. How could I have forgotten on
Sunday . . . oh yes, that hurricane has me quite scattered . . . you
sure state my predicament. Our friends in California are trying to
lure us over there to some vegan animation paradise, but I don't
want to leave the south. My mama's heart is already nearly broke
that I don't live in Columbia and I don't want to move way way
far away from her.

Paul left this morning to drive to Baton Rouge, hoping to get
into New Orleans tomorrow and see if our cats made it. Lolis
Elie rescued cats from 2 or 3 houses in Mid-City yesterday
and they were all ALIVE. I sure could use a hurricane mirâcle.
I am absolutely dying to see it all . . . but I've got a nursing baby
attached to me and I don't want him anywhere near the city.
I've been waiting and hoping Paul would go, and he's finally
gonna give it a try. I'm afraid he has quite an aversion and is not

one to want to row around and look but I'll see if he could have a
look at your house . . . They say it is easy to get in, but it may be
hard to get out!?

I couldn't believe it. That was it. The final straw. Nothing
against Paul, but Paul was from Canada. A naturalized Louisianan would be back in my city before I was? No way. If Paul was
going, I was going.

see ya, wouldn't want to be ya

More than a few friends who were renters suddenly announced they were bailing on their flooded New Orleans lives for Brooklyn or Chicago or metropolitan wherever. Like it was good while it lasted, y'all, but see ya, wouldn't want to be ya. Never looking back wasn't so much an option, even if you wanted it to be, if you had a house you were still paying for.

I think Jake saw his nearly finished second album for the Wisconsin weirdo's micro-label spontaneously combust. Or drown. On a satellite photo on the Internet we had seen the submerged top of his white touring van in front of our house glowing like an egg in a murky cup of coffee.

Not that disintegration wasn't often at hand when dealing with musicians, mood disorders, girlfriends, hiatuses, and low-budget van touring. Things could be going swimmingly, then all of a sudden how one guy handed another guy a French fry or double-soloed on his vocoder could change everything. Jake had other irons in the fire, but music was the iron he had loved and polished for years.

I couldn't not look back. What Bourbon Street megaphone preachers always embellished into Sodom and Gomorrah was home. Besides, no one I knew in their cramped apartments in other cities had anything. But the angel trumpet flower tree I planted in our yard long ago had quickly blossomed into a huge kinetic sculpture, strange and sulky. I could prune it back to a memory and, within months, the fertile soil would make its umbrella pop wide again. I had rampant vines of purple spaceship passiflora and a blooming bird-of-paradise, for God's sake. One summer night when our friend's jazz trio played at the Dragon's Den, the sky had opened up. A soft gray curtain enveloped the balcony, rain-charging the air and sealing us in with the music. For so many reasons, I wasn't ready to *c'est la vie*. We needed to see for ourselves how irrevocable our old life really was.

Some people Uptown were still holed up with their guns and provisions, and the Quarter was dry. If there was anything of ours left, we wanted it before the mold or someone took it. I did not want to be washed up in metropolitan wherever with just our dogs and skivvies. I was no frothing property rights type, but being told we could not access our own property for weeks did not seem exactly American. Yet what had preceded it did not seem American, either.

Since Nola was still under martial law and they would not open our flooded but mostly drained zip code to us for re-entry, we were left with the weird problem of how to sneak back to our own house. On websites I read stuff like *be warned if your house flooded you will be electrocuted if you so much as touch it!!!* (which I doubted) and *I went back into Mid-City Friday with a pass and a police escort. I saw two men walking down the street who were promptly arrested by the nopd. If you don't look "official" be prepared for jail* (which I did not).

The Nola-lockouts grapevine said we could get into the city if we hiked in along River Road carless or if we put some medical scrubs like the keytar player in an old Prince video and faked our way in. I did not want to impersonate a doctor or even an EMT. I didn't care whose friend's cousin had scored with this. Search-and-rescue was still on, and parts of town still had water. I was extremely wary, even terrified, of messing with sleep-

deprived, possibly unhinged members of the NOPD. NOPD bru-
tality scandals were so commonplace as to barely rate as scandals.
Now many of their houses had flooded, too.

I e-mailed an old editor friend who was kind enough to fax
us press passes so we could get to our house. I warned him that I
didn't think I could write anything. I had been working on a revi-
sion of a novel, and my agent e-mailed to check that I had gotten
out. I e-mailed back something about a three-week setback, hoping that was the case.

Because it was Louisiana, there was a steady buzz about bribes.
I was kindly advised from the 504, 985, and 225 area codes that
freedom of the press was fine and dandy for those silly enough
to think they had it, but not to hold my breath. I should forget
the First Amendment way, and go back to the Louisiana way.
Bribing.

With all the unsolicited payola advice I was receiving, you
would think I was trying to get Edwin Edwards to steer a highway
contract my way instead of just getting my belongings from my
soaked house. I was told I must pack cartons of cigarettes and iced
Igloos of Gatorade for National Guardsmen sweating at highway
checkpoints in steamy, ninety-plus heat. From a liquor-marketing
guy in Baton Rouge, the Southern wine and spirits industrial complex weighed in with a disturbing blend of corporate psychology
and racial profiling. Pressing a case of tiny sample liquor bottles
into my friends' hands, he advised, "Courvoisier is for the *black*
soldiers. Tequila is for *whites.*"

While I was busy mocking the Rambos, bits of their survival-
ist mantra somehow colonized a corner of my mind. We got hepatitis A and B and tetanus shots and planned to incarcerate Buster
and Clo in Mississippi. Soon we were in the Salvation Army store
buying discarded sheriff T-shirts and cargo pants.

Formerly the kind of people who signed petitions against
Wal-Mart's labor practices and planned invasion of the historic

Lower Garden District, suddenly Jake and I had brand-new Sam's Club cards blazing in our expedition pants pockets. We bought huge bags of dog food because we had heard about the stranded survivor packs. Soon we had rubber boots, Hazmat gear, tools, industrial-size jars of peanut butter and hand sanitizer, and water, water, water weighing down the back of Jack's mini-pickup. Worried about our finances, I could not believe we had to spend money on all this disaster crap. Packing unwanted provisions and two haggard hound dogs under the red truck's topper, I barely recognized us.

The plan, such as it was, was multipronged. Be prepared to show our press passes and, in case they didn't work, dress vaguely emergency-style and know several ways to sneak in. Because my mom kept telling me it wasn't safe for females, I stopped calling her and bought a baseball cap.

Heading back, I looked over at Jake in his ugly new clothes manning the wheel of the truck and thought, Good old Jake.

Jake was flexible. He had a knack for rising or lowering to the occasion as required. Jake would be my secret weapon. I wasn't sure what I would be.

"If I have to be flooded, then I'm . . ." I said.

"If?" Jake interrupted.

"If I have to be flooded"—I continued—"and it looks like I do . . . there's no one I'd rather be flooded with."

"Thanks," Jake said. "I guess."

I looked at myself in the truck's side mirror. I still had my bookish glasses, but I had stuffed my shoulder-length hair into my new baseball cap to screw up my courage. I looked stupid but also determined. Like the hat helped. Jake glanced over.

"You look like a lesbian," he said.

Packed bumper to bumper with displaced people and disaster trucks, and most of the pine trees scattered or snapped, Hattiesburg looked like a totally different town. Some buildings were smushed like white bread. I was surprised that a town two hours away from both the Gulf Coast and New Orleans looked so screwed.

"Brad said they've got an electrician coming, so hopefully they'll have power back. Also they're spraying for the fleas that took over. He apologizes in advance if we get bit," I said. "He also said his band is playing Saturday. If we're back he'll get us in for free and buy us some sympathy beers."

"I doubt we'll be doing that."

"Maybe," I said.

I had gone to a street festival in Mississippi a few months before and saw Brad's band play songs about aliens and getting drunk on love. I could barely picture myself now in the sun wearing a tank top and drinking lemonade, watching old ladies smoke cigarettes. At a makeshift FEMA center at a Mississippi church, we had just attended our own strange induction ceremony: some drawn churchmen instructed us to sign here and there and somberly presented us with a folded tarp.

Dropping the dogs off at the Mississippi kennel sucked, partially because it meant admitting that New Orleans wasn't fit for a dog. And yet. For the same price in New Orleans, instead of a cramped concrete pen, Buster and Clo had boarded at Phydeaux's, where they lounged on a futon with a hippie lady and some dissolute Uptown dogs. With the Mississippi warden leading them off, Buster jogged dumbly enthused to his cell block.

But Clo locked her front legs and put on the brakes, cutting her fogged, sclerotic eyes over her shoulders at me in alarm. Clo had been a reasonable sport for the past few weeks. She had submitted to frequent paw scrubbing and garage confinement, as well as occasionally letting me cry into her fur. Until we took them out of Jack's pickup and she heard the frantic barking, I think she thought we were on our way home.

"Suck it up and be glad you're not barking on a roof some-where," I told her.

When we got to Brad and Sam's house, we saw that some trees had smashed their carport and car. We picked our way around some huge, freshly split pine trunks and went inside.

"We thought it was hitting y'all," Brad said.

"We thought it was hitting *y'all*," I said.

"Then we thought it was just hitting the coast," Brad said.

"We wound up in the hallway crying under a mattress!" Sam said.

I liked Sam. She had a beautiful voice and worked at the Social Security office and still had the energy to cut a CD and gig around in bars. She had only one hand yet had danced for the Rebellettes dance team at Ole Miss. They made her practice highkicks until she got lipstick on her knees. I felt bad that she and Brad had wound up in that hallway hunkered down Mom-style.

They still looked startled.

"No offense, but I'm sure glad I'm not y'all," Brad said.

"Yeah, well. Anytime," I said. "There's a lot of people right now I'm glad not to be."

Jake just shrugged.

"What are y'all going to *do*?" Sam said.

Jake started saying stuff. Brad showed Jake his new bass. Mostly I sat on the sofa and tried to follow, but I was beat. And I was getting weirded out at the way Brad and Sam sat smiling at us, grins posted ear to ear. With their somewhat smashed house and totaled car, their situation did not strike me as awesome. But there they were, grinning and almost giddy. It was the euphoria of near-missitis. They were thrilled to be alive.

The next morning, our passes worked like a charm. No back-room deals required. But there were smells. Before we even got into New Orleans we could smell it.

When we left New Orleans, everything was green and bursting; now everything was brown and dead. I had never been in New Orleans or any other city alone. The city looked like make-believe. Like a movie about zombies and a nuclear war.

"We're the only people here," I said.

"I know," Jake said, clutching the wheel.

"There are supposedly people downtown," I said.

"It's creepy," Jake agreed. "Let's not talk about it."

Every street the great sewer had flowed in and out of was now a dirt road. We were dumb and had entered the city in a bad way. Now we were taking side roads around downed power lines, floated cars, and pancaked houses. Occasionally we cruised past a marooned boat. A pack of feral dogs and a poodle with a grown-out shag raced past. We stopped and dumped a bag of food in case they galloped back by.

On the way to our house in this browned make-believe, a figure appeared on a porch. There stood a slight, elderly woman all alone.

"What the hell?" Jake asked.

"I do not know," I said.

"They said they got everybody," Jake said.

We stopped the truck. Boots crunching the crusted sidewalk as we walked toward her in the early-morning gloom, we must have looked ominous. She edged closer to her open front door. I took off my baseball cap and waved.

"Hi," I said. "We live over that way by Banks. How are you?"

"Holding up," she said in a shaky voice. "Water's down now."

"Has it been down long?" Jake said.

"Few days," she said, squinting. "I ran out of batteries for my radio. But the power should be on soon."

A thin and raggedy-looking German shepherd mix peered out of the open front door.

"I see you've got a friend," I said.

"Oh, that's Karma. He didn't like that water. Not one bit. That's for sure. I stayed up on the dresser and he stayed up on the table and he'd do pretty good."

"For how long?" I said.

"Just a few days. I feel bad for those people who *really* flooded. I got *lucky*. I just got some. He'd go down and do his business in the water and then climb back up and sleep and eat on his table. Up and down, up and down, like that. Then Karma had enough with that water. He bit me, didn't you honey? He couldn't help it."

She held out her arm and showed me a purpling wound.

"Ouch," I said.

"I washed it good," she said. "I'm Ann."

"Cheryl," I said.

"Jake," Jake said.

I glanced over at Jake. He was staring at the dog bite. It looked infected. Jake's face had a look I had never seen before.

"Karma sure is good looking," I said.

Karma was actually a little wild-looking. It was weeks after the hurricane. I wondered when he had last eaten and hoped he did not come down off that porch.

"I don't think they're going to be getting the power back on for a while yet," Jake ventured.

Miss Ann seemed to consider this. "It could be another day or two, I guess," she said.

"The news said it's not going to be a few days," I said. "They're not letting people back in this part of town yet."

"You're back," she said.

"Yeah, but just during the day. We're not spending the night. No one else is coming back for weeks probably. Aren't y'all hot?"

"A little," she admitted. "But we sit out here and get our little breeze and we do okay."

"I wouldn't want to be here by myself," I said. "I hate to think of you here by yourself."

"I'm not by myself," she said. "I'm here with Karma."

"You have any supplies left?" Jake asked. "Any water?"

"I have a few cans of food. A little water. Karma's running low on dog food."

"Can we give you a ride somewhere, Miss Ann?" I said.

She stiffened. "I already talked to the National Guard. They can't *make* you leave."

"True," I said. "But did they tell you they had free places to stay though until they get the power back? Until you can come home."

"Oh, I don't know about all that."

"I'm going to get you some water," Jake said. "And we have extra dog food."

"Oh, I don't want to be any trouble. What about you and your husband?"

"We have enough. We're leaving tonight," I said.

"I wouldn't feel right taking your water," she said. "But a little dog food would help."

"We brought extra in case anybody needed it. My feelings would be really hurt if you did not take it. I would be worried about Karma all night."

Jake came back from the truck with the stuff. He handed some to her and put the rest on the porch.

"All right," she said, looking a little teary. "*Thank* you."

"Miss Ann, do you need to call anybody? Somebody might be worried about you."

"My niece. But I don't have her number."

"Tell me her name and where she lives and we'll find it," I said. "We're going to come back and bring you some batteries and more water tomorrow."

We got back in the car. Jake swung the car around some metal warehouses shredded into the street. He was shaking his head.

"What?" I said.

"Just everything," he said.

"Please don't step on any wires," I said. "I'm begging you."

"I'm not. They're over there," Jake said, pointing to the power lines drooped to the sidewalk.

Nothing was the same as we had left it. My fleshy century plant had collapsed to goo, like a dead octopus someone slung into my yard. The white picket fence was bent and missing teeth and looked like someone had smeared it with a dirty diaper. My red bottlebrush tree was brown and broken across our front steps. Our oranges had shriveled on the branch. A child's plastic tricycle had floated onto our porch.

Jake's van was soupy and sealed shut. He pulled at the handle a few times and started karate-kicking it. I already had on my rubber boots. I put on my gloves. I had vowed not to touch anything with my bare hands that had touched that stink water. I tried to wrestle the tree off the front porch. Jake's roundhousing echoed across the empty blocks.

"It has to open," he said, delivering another mean kick.

"Oh Lord," I said. "Don't break your foot. Why do you need it to open? It'll probably stink and then we won't be able to get it back shut."

Jake panted.

"I . . . just . . . do!" he puffed, kicking.

Our house was raised on three-foot piers, but the water had risen higher than Jake's van. I hadn't realized our house was so crooked until I saw the slime line all around it. For some reason, a house across the street that was also on piers seemed flooded a little less. When had we sunk so low?

The wind had carved two dollhouses on our block—sheared their back walls completely off. You could see an empty bed and dresser in the upstairs bedroom of the elderly couple's house on the corner. The other dollhouse in our backyard, above what used to be our shed, had a little second-story kitchen open to the sky.

Jake gave up on his van and started on our swollen front door. Once he pried it open, we strapped on our gas masks and took our first moonwalk. A thick coating of mud slicked the floors. Furniture had floated and tipped. Our armchairs were fatter than they'd been before we left, swollen like water balloons and thick with blue-black mold fuzz. It would all have been very interesting if it hadn't happened to us.

The roof was skinned to the tar paper. It had flooded downstairs and rained water and glass upstairs. The wind had rattled or blown in most of our upstairs windows. It had ripped siding from the front and back and sides and then punched holes through our plaster. Fleeing roaches died glued to walls at the top of the waterline. Maggots and brown water and dog food churned in the tipped fridge. We found a tiny, bleating frog.

Seeing sodden walls and wood floors bursting at the seams with moist sewage and ruined effort, I was sorry I had spent all spring and summer working so hard on the house. If New Orleans was going to disintegrate around me, why had I painted and scraped so much? I wished instead that I had taken more dog walks and gone to hear our friend play his vibes more often. I should have gone every single day to the Vietnamese market to buy green coconuts and fat pink straws for coco frios.

We were going to take all of our salvageable stuff to a storage unit Mom had found in Hammond. It was a tiny space, the only one she could find, and I had been obsessing that it would not hold everything. Now I knew it would be too big; we only had a few things left.

"Check it out," Jake said, turning a new electric guitar upside down. Water trickled out.

"I'm sorry," I said.

He shrugged. "Help me drag this out," he said. "I don't want to dump it in here."

A large plastic bin brimmed with nasty black water. It was choking me even through the mask. I gagged. Floating in the swill was Jake's band's CDs and seven-inch records and years of show fliers he or the guys or I had made. We dumped it down the front steps.

I was tossing my life to the curb and wondering how much clean water we would have to truck in to even begin to bleach the sludge off the floor, when I saw two bedraggled figures picking through some sewage-soaked garbage half a block away. The zombie set had sprung to life.

A slouching old woman with a long gray ponytail and a teen picked through a trash can that had floated and spilled. I recognized the teenager. He was a tall, pale, developmentally disabled kid with matted curly hair. I had been worried a few months ear lier when I saw him shuffling around the streets of Mid-City in his pajamas and slippers.

I called out and motioned them over. The old woman shook her head no and kept digging in the garbage, but the teenager took a few tentative steps. He met me halfway in the middle of the deserted street. I took off my mask and we looked at each other. I did not know what to say.

"Do you want a Coke or some water?" I asked.

The boy nodded. He was clutching the top of his pants so they would not slide off. He was a lot thinner than when I had seen him earlier that summer. I did not understand why the rescuers had not gotten to everyone yet.

"Where do you live?"

He pointed down the street to the right side of the next block.

"Do you know y'all can go to a shelter?" I asked. "I would be happy to give you a ride."

"My aunt won't," he said.

"Would you like me to talk to her?"

"She *won't*," he said.

"Y'all have any food?" I said.

He leaned closer as if his aunt had supersonic hearing.

"We had some bread before the storm," he whispered.

"Hold on," I said.

I jogged over to our borrowed truck and brought back candy bars, crackers, and water. I hoped all the junk food on top of no food did not make him sick.

Later that day, we met Mom at a truckstop in Hammond near the storage unit. She sat dejected across from me in a molded plastic booth and watched me drink a Big Gulp. I didn't have anything to say.

"Y'all are going *back?* I don't see what you need to go back in there for," Mom fussed.

"We have to throw out more stuff. We need to bleach the walls and stop the mold."

"I just don't think it's safe," Mom said.

"There's nobody there," I said.

"That's what's unsafe. And who *knows* what else." She turned to Jake. "Do you think it's safe?" she demanded.

"Safe enough," he shrugged.

"I brought this," Mom said. She fished a saint scapula out of her purse and leaned across the table to hang it around my neck.

"Thanks," I said.

"You need to get that woman's niece on the phone to get her to talk some sense into her," Mom said. "She's not in her right mind. Can't be. Hold the phone up to her ear if you have to. And just tell some police about that family. They're supposed to have military in there. Go find them. You can't help everybody."

"Why didn't we do that instead of just giving them the rest of our food?" I said.

"Because the aunt won't let him leave. Because it was getting dark," Jake said. "There wasn't anybody."

We went to buy more food and water for Miss Ann and the forgotten family, some bleach for our walls, and another tarp and some nails for our roof. We pulled up at Mom's house exhausted.

Lori was chubby and in her thirties; she had a pixie cut and a round, young face. Though I'm eleven months older and spent my entire childhood taking care of her, she likes to boss me. When we got inside, she followed close at my heels shaking a finger and scolding.

"What happen your house? What happen your house, Cherra? Your house messed up! You gone spend the night and spend the night and spend the night. *I know.* You move in. I said *you . . . move . . . IN!*"

"Stop fussing. You're living the high life. You're lucky," I told her, thinking of the poor developmentally disabled guy we'd left in the street.

After some Web searching, I found the phone number for Miss Ann's niece. I called her.

"You don't know me, but I am calling because I saw your aunt in New Orleans today," I said.

The woman burst into tears.

Around the city, there was heartbreaking garbage clotting the interstates. Toys, clothes, mattresses. My eyes could not get used to it.

In Mid-City the next morning, Miss Ann was sitting on her porch stroking Karma and waving a new carton of cigarettes.

"A nice police lady brought me these," she said, shaking them in the air like a maraca. "Very sweet girl. Officer Penny. She said she's coming back by to see me."

"Your niece really wants to talk to you," I said. "They've been looking for you. They're worried sick."

Miss Ann's niece had said her aunt was nearly eighty and stubborn. I dialed the niece and handed Miss Ann my cell phone. Jake and I brought in water and a few bags of groceries. After a few minutes, Miss Ann handed me back the phone. She seemed embarrassed.

"Thank you so much," she said. "I hate to have people so *worried*."

"We would love to take you somewhere with a shower and a bed," I said again. "They're putting people up for free."

"Then I'll miss Officer Penny," she said.

I wondered if Miss Ann was lying. Officer Penny sounded suspiciously made up, like a character with a two-foot tinfoil badge on a Pee Wee Herman show. But then there were the mysterious cigarettes. They had to have come from somewhere. I had wanted to break through her hold-out denial but now it seemed like by bringing supplies we had bolstered some batty defenses. Her dog bite looked like it needed a doctor.

"I'm worried because you've been out here like this for weeks now. I don't know how you're going to keep getting water," I said. "I promise you this Winn Dixie is not opening and the power isn't coming back on this week."

"Probably not this month," Jake added. "And we're leaving in a few days."

"I'll talk to Officer Penny," she said. "We thank you so much. Karma thanks you, too. Boy, he had himself a good supper last night."

When we brought the wandering family the groceries, the teen clapped his hands. But his hunched aunt came to the door and asked if I had brought any sugar; she had used all of hers making sweet tea with the contaminated water from her tap. They were camped out in their unflooded upstairs.

The aunt took the bags, but wouldn't look me in the eye. At first I thought she was scared cagey or still storm-shocked;

then I realized she was mentally ill. That's why the boy was wandering in his pajamas a few months ago. New Orleans often tore at your heart like that. A lot of people moved away after their eyes burned from seeing one more sad or neglectful thing. Over the years I've taken home my share of babies in diapers who had toddled a block or two alone—sometimes back to a six- or seven-year-old who had been left in charge. So I could believe that people lived this terribly. What I couldn't believe was that even after the flood and the thousands of broken pipes, this woman still had water.

"Listen, y'all shouldn't drink that tap water," I tried to explain. "It's really bad for you. Use this water we brought. They said on TV that the tap water can make you sick now. Very sick. The pipes got dirty with the flood."

She shook her head.

"Tastes fine," she said. "Let it run awhile. It's good. Good tea."

I went back to the car and slammed the door.

"What?" Jake said.

"We need to send somebody," I said.

"They won't go," he said.

"I don't care. They're like kids in there."

On the way back to our own mess, we drove a few blocks over by Paul and Helen's, hoping Paul or anyone normal to talk to would still be in the zombiescape. Of course he wasn't. No one was. He had come and left.

But around the corner from Paul and Helen's house, a guy with a video camera stood on the neutral ground in the middle of the eerie, mud-craterscape. It was like seeing a spaceman.

"Wait. I think that's Bill," Jake said. "This guy I worked with."

"What?" I said. "What in the world is he doing?"

"I have no clue," Jake said, pulling to a stop near him.

The camera guy stepped slightly closer, peering at the people in the truck nervously.

"It's Jake," Jake hollered.

"Oh my God!" The guy smiled. "Weird. I haven't seen a single person."

"What are you doing?" Jake said.

"Shooting this documentary. This guy holed up with about a dozen or so animals and is still here. What are you doing?"

"Our house," Jake said.

"Yeah," the guy said. "Well. Good luck."

"Right," Jake replied.

We drove back the four filthy blocks through the ruinscape that had been our neighborhood, going the wrong way up one-way streets to avoid split trees, milky-brown flooded cars, collapsed and scattered brick walls, and power lines. The stench and a bed-sheet rope twisted out an attic window got to me. I hoped we did not get a flat tire.

"A documentary?" I said. "Fuck that guy. Look at this place."

The government ordered a mandatory evacuation for Hurricane Rita, and the next morning our press passes did not work. An exhausted, red-eyed New Orleans police officer turned us away as "nonessentials." I did not have the heart to talk First Amendment and I did not have any tequila or Courvoisier. Blocking the recently drained Metairie Road, dwarfed by early-morning fog and the overpass, the policeman cut a sad figure—tiny and alone, like he was propped against a toy cop car.

As we snuck in another way, the probability of another huge hurricane heading straight to our house seemed unfathomable, yet strangely possible. Maybe my worldview was being rearranged on a subatomic level. All of a sudden longshot odds didn't seem quite so long. Like we should start playing Louisiana Lotto.

"If it floods again now, it might not matter," I said. "It might wash it out some."

Jake gave me a crazy look. "If this hits, it better blow this shit down. I don't want it to flood again," he said, like it was a matter of principle.

As we were unloading our supplies, an out-of-town ambulance dragged slowly up our street, the first emergency vehicle we had seen. We flagged it down. The driver told us we needed to leave. We pointed the ambulance crew to the wandering family and told them about the mentally ill aunt who would not let the increasingly skinny teen leave. Soon a police cruiser, a Humvee, and an ambulance converged on the family and their flood poisoned sweet tea, whisking them away.

The roof was mostly tar paper and slick. Going out there seemed like a bad idea. I remembered the evacuation boarding-up. A fat lot of good it did. From my blown-out back window I could see skinned roofs all the way to downtown. No other couples were out on their roofs tarping. Having fought somewhat of a fight, I was now half prepared to join everyone else and surrender myself to the futility of it all and whatever happened after futility.

Not Jake. He was too mad. He refused to believe that people could keep getting slapped around week after week, unable to change the crappy course of anything. It was either an insane or defining moment. Or both.

"The wind is going to rip this off," I said.

"Not if we do it right," Jake said. "Do you want it to keep raining inside?"

"If it's going to flood again, I don't care," I said.

"If it doesn't, we'll never get rid of the mold. All the work we did this week will be ruined."

Since I was lazy and had already sorted through the sodden remains of a whole summer's ruined renovations, Jake had struck a nerve.

"Okay," I said. I slung a leg out the window and ventured onto our roof's steep incline. "But I'm staying on this side by the window."

We were half done when an NOPD cruiser pulled up and stopped in the middle of our street.

"What do you think you're doing?" a voice called up.

Another voice joined the first.

"We're going to have to see some ID."

Jake reflexively reached for his wallet, which wasn't there. It was on the floor of the borrowed truck. "Be right down," he called politely.

"No way," I said.

Jake pounded a few extra tacks in quickly. I edged over to the window and climbed inside.

"Motherfucker," Jake said, falling into the upstairs bedroom window behind me.

"Ooh, watch that broken glass," I said. "A lot of looters must tarp the roof as a favor on their way out."

"No shit," Jake said. "I do not want to deal with this."

He took a deep breath. Jake didn't trust the NOPD ever since that delusional, disabled veteran—the Raid Man who kept all the insecticide cans arranged like voodoo on his front porch underneath a yellowing poster of former mayor Marc Morial—had fixated on Jake and Buster and brought two NOPD officers to our front door. "That's him! That's him! That's the dog! That's the tattoo!" he had cried when we answered the stern knock. "You're going to walk before the judge!"

The officers tried not to laugh when they saw the killer basset and the bespectacled guy, but Jake fit the vague description of the hooligan who had supposedly pushed Raid Man down. Buster was a dog and Jake was white with glasses and a tattoo. So the officers cuffed Jake and drove him around in the back of their squad car to appease the Raid Man, then snuck him back home and dusted him off. Problem solved.

But these officers were too beat for illegal detentions. They checked our IDs and told us Rita was coming and to leave as soon as we were through. We climbed back out the window and finished, but it was getting late. Then we couldn't find the key to the truck. We looked everywhere. I kept thinking about the leaky levees.

"Let's give it half an hour more then start walking downtown," I said. "We need to go before it gets dark so maybe someone can give us a ride out."

Finally, Jake spotted the keys on the floorboard of the locked truck. "Shit," he said. "This is that cop's fault for freaking me out."

"It's okay," I said. "At least we found it. We can break the window if we need to."

"It's Jack's truck."

"Yeah, he'd really want us stuck here."

"I'm going to at least try not to break it first," Jake said.

We got a coat hanger and a rusty screwdriver out of the house and each got to work on a different door. I heard a motor in the distance. Because the city was deserted, you could hear cars coming from half a mile away. A few minutes later, a brand-new Cadillac with no license plate cruised up and stopped. Jake gave me the worst look. It was New Orleans. Fifty-fifty we were about to be mugged or helped. A thin, older man we had never seen before got out. He leaned against his new Cadillac and sighed, watching us.

I nodded hello. He was not one of our neighbors. Why was he here? Was he bored? Did he want something? Was he an "essential person"? Was he lonely? Could we take him if we had to? Why would we have to? His car was brand new and nicer than ours. He wasn't leaving. He just stood there watching.

"Locked out," the man finally pronounced. "That's a shame."

After watching us in silence a few more minutes, he opened his trunk. "I got this," he said, producing a shiny metal jimmy. The news kept raving about all those stolen Cadillacs from Sewell's. I told myself not to be paranoid. Just because this guy had a jimmy in the empty trunk of a new Cadillac didn't mean this car was one of them.

He handed the jimmy to Jake just as his cell phone rang. The man answered it.

"I'm standing here right now," he said. "No one broke in. Your front door's shut. It's all wet, but it's shut. I can't do that. No, I cannot. I'm standing here telling you how much water it was, baby. I don't want any trouble. You're burning up my minutes. I'ma give you to this man here. Your neighbor. He'll tell you."

He handed Jake the phone. "She don't want to believe me," he said to me.

"Hello. Hi. Yeah, well, it's about like he said. No, I can't kick it in. I'm sorry. NOPD was just by here asking for my ID for being on my own roof. I wouldn't have anywhere to put it anyway. I'm sorry. Very sorry. I'm gonna give you back to your friend now."

"See, I told you," the old man said.

"Her stuff," Jake said, reapplying himself to the jimmy.

Maybe because everything was surreal, the crew wearing FDNY gear seemed fake when they pulled up. They waved bottles of drinking water at us from the back of a pick-up. With their Village People mustaches and swagger and Brooklyn-movie accents, here they suddenly were in post-apocalyptic Nola on our very own zombie set.

"Who needs water?" one of them asked.

"We're locked out of our car," I said.

They helped Jake lift the topper off the back and assessed the situation. One of them tried to pry Jack's back window open. It promptly shattered.

"Way to go," one of the firemen said.

"Oops," another one said.

Someone laughed.

"That's one way," some other guy said.

"I don't know who can fit through there," the fireman who broke the window said.

The shattered window was only the size of a few shoeboxes. Everyone looked at me. I didn't want my stomach cut up. One of the firemen got a cloth and spread it over the glass.

"Okay," I said. "Somebody hold my feet."

Sitting in some crunchy glass as we headed out of town, I was grateful yet unimpressed.

"We could have busted out this back window ourselves an hour ago," I said. "I thought FDNY is supposed to be all badass. I hope Jack isn't mad we messed up his truck."

"Who cares," Jake says. "I don't give a *fuck*."

That didn't sound like Jake, but it was.

I didn't know that you could leave your house one person and return another. That the planets can shift to suddenly make you four or five people all at once, none slightly resembling who you thought you were before. I did not start this summer as a haphazard victim, rescuer, roofer, or adventurer. I hated swashbucklers.

Our trip had confirmed the worst plus some. Our little world had been obliterated. What would happen was hard to imagine. I was not hundreds of books and a desk and a garden. And Jake was not a bunch of records and recording software and instruments. And yet stripped raw of everything you felt naked. Like maybe your ass was showing.

happy cheese town far, far away

The water got on everything. Thousands who didn't flood lost their jobs. Thousands of others were told not to come back to work for three or four months, or to report to work in another town. Still others got the pleasure of firing flooded friends before being fired or forced into early retirement.

Other people were the only relatives left dry and thus had lost family members suddenly marooned on their sofas and floors. Still others were left alone in New Orleans now after all their friends and family had been forced out—no one left to have a cup of coffee with once the power came back on. In the great suffering equation, these were the *good* fates—all far preferable to drowning or having a heatstroke on the interstate on-ramp waiting for rescue. These dead neighbors hung in the air like chiding ghosts; every time another poor aunt or uncle was discovered in or under a flooded house, these ghosts chattered and everyone raged and shivered.

It was *beyond* beyond the pale, and hundreds of thousands of people did not have a clue. Whoever said they did was lying.

Some people, flooded and not, after a month's miserable forced vacation, had spent a lot of time doing some dangerous thinking. These folks decided their New Orleans lives were shit, a death wish, a dreamy slacker dream, or never worth their fabulous selves or their children's tuition money to begin with. So sayonara, baby. I had never seen so many people hastily implementing so many seat-of-the-pants plans in my life.

I'm going to Brooklyn to work in a belt buckle factory. I think it will be a Good Experience for my artsy New Orleans middle schooler to see what it's like to go to a wealthy Episcopal school in Delaware for a few months. My job is moving to Baton Rouge and, you know I've always despised Baton Rouge, but maybe it's not so bad. These were the kinds of things I heard. Along with *I just sold my two flooded houses for the price of a used car each and I'm moving to West Virginia. And I'm following my drummer to Chicago.*

So many smart people sounded so blindsided every time they opened their mouths that I worried I was one of them. Well-meaning out-of-town friends called my GoPhone with absurd suggestions of where Jake and I should stow ourselves. Austin, Asheville, and Portland kept coming up as our personal Shangri-La for reasons I could not fathom other than that these were towns with well-documented vegetarian populations. Why not invest in some silicon and move to Orange County instead? Or have a captain of finance and wife makeover and head for Connecticut? It was just as random. Someone thought we would make good substitute teachers.

I was getting irritated with people's lame suggestions. It wasn't true that any life, just pick-a-life, would be better than a New Orleans life. But I also realized that no one we knew had ever had everything around them change all at once. Of total upheaval, they and we had happily known nothing. Now we knew an ounce more. Everyone whose lives had been touched by the ruining water was already a fumbling expert. It was on-the-job training.

Hearing foolishness on top of craziness, and seeing that our mayor and governor were just beginning to wipe the tears from their eyes, it occurred to me that maybe no one was in any condition to decide anything. Our plan wasn't much of a plan—stop the mold before it really got started, meet with the insurance people if they would ever come, and then decide what to do next. Take a month to see whether our freelance work survived. Sign no leases with money we might not have. Sleep where we could. Try not to go willy-nilly. Hug it out. Wait and see.

Wait and see meant staying. A few days later, Rita creamed Cameron Parish and reflooded a good bit of New Orleans, but thankfully not us again. We were back watching a friend's Uptown house. It was hot. The house didn't flood but had no usable water or electricity. It had a leaking slate roof, moldy ceilings, and a putrid duct-taped refrigerator that Buster and Clo kept sniffing. We felt lucky to be there.

In exchange for the roof and door that locked could we please, please drive to Gentilly and break into my friend's tattoo-artist-son's flooded house? She'd forced her music-buff husband to store most of his record collection there on the second floor. And now look. Marriages had been ruined by far, far less. Could we pretty please get the collection before the mold did?

"O-kaaay," I agreed on the phone. "But you better not get me arrested. They're driving around looking for looters."

"If the police come, just call me and I'll say I gave you permission."

"It's soldiers with rifles in Humvees," I said. "I don't know if they want to talk to someone's mom."

In Gentilly, our boots kept getting stuck in some kind of two-foot muck from the canal break.

"This is a really bad idea," I said, lacing my fingers together behind my knees and hoisting my feet free.

"No shit," Jake replied.

We hurled a brick through the back door's window, unlocked it, then tried in vain to turn the doorknob. Finally, Jake kicked it in. As he ferried armloads of records to the car around the goo pit while I stood lookout, no one rolled up to stop us. I decided we should not leave our new replacement tools at our own flooded house.

Because we were back, word had spread that we were the hook-up. Our phone started ringing with other sad requests we might blow yet could not refuse. We'd already failed to rescue a friend's mom's cat. We'd gone to check out friends' houses to report back on how screwed they were. I was hoping that if there was a great karma bank it all got deposited there, because it looked like we might be requiring regular withdrawals.

A jazz historian in Metairie had let us strip to our rubber boots and hose down in his backyard, and he certainly didn't have to. Weirdly, a cousin of Tanio's, a 9-11 widow named Katrina whom we had never met, sent word that she wanted to pay back people's kindnesses to her. She said that she could arrange for us to stay in an empty house in upstate New York that was the home of Velveeta. I hoped to God not to take her up on it. But sweating under a mosquito netting while the dogs panted pitifully and flies buzzed the maggoty fridge in the next room, thinking about a happy life in a happy cheese town far, far away made me feel better.

We had made the mistake of driving the entire city end to end to see what had happened. Now all the degradation film-looped on the back of my eyelids when I shut my eyes at night. Bedtime brought itchy wet heat and images of escape holes people had hacked in their roofs.

Jake and I weren't getting along the best we ever had, either. We'd get along fine tossing out stuff and bleaching our floors in gas-masked but amicable silence in ghastlyville all day, then come back Uptown and squabble like twelve-year-olds under a miserable, torn mosquito net at night. It was all "scoot over no you scoot over my arm's hanging out getting bit shut up no you shut up no really shhhh whatwasthatnoise?"

It was unnerving being the only people on the block. One

night we invited a friend over to have no lights with us so we would all be less scared and blue.

"We've got SpaghettiO's and bean dip," I bragged on the phone, knowing these were luxuries.

"And salsa," Jake said. "And Blue Runner red beans."

"What's Jake saying?" Kelly said.

"He said y'all come on over," I said. "We're bored and freaking ourselves out."

Kelly was a big reader who always seemed to have a new girlfriend. She had dirty blond hair, librarian glasses, and a Georgia accent. She did not look like the top hat type who gave haunted French Quarter tours, but she did. Soon she was knocking at our front door in the pitch black with a dog and a bearded twenty-something roommate.

"I had to get back. People in Georgia were looking at me. I could not go anywhere without getting the evil eye," she said. "I'm like, have you people never seen a lesbian?"

"That's ridiculous. They've got plenty of lesbians in Georgia," I said. "They've even got plenty of lesbians in Mississippi."

"I know," she said.

"What did you have on?" I said.

"Nothing special. Like this," she said, pointing to her wife-beater-style tank top and shorts.

"Those clothes are normal for New Orleans," I agreed. "They're normal for any city actually."

"I *know*," she said.

"How is it down by your house?" Jake asked. "You didn't flood, right?"

Kelly lived across town in the New Marigny, what she called *the shooting side of St. Claude*. The bearded twenty-something cleared his throat from the gloomy recesses of our candlelit living room.

"You don't want to know," he grumbled.

"Yes, I do," I said.

"Well you're not even going to believe this shit," Kelly said, launching into a terrifying tale about an emaciated pit bull and a chain. At the end of it, she and the bearded guy were both crying and Jake had turned his head. I felt queasy. I wondered if she still thought it was worth getting out of Georgia to come back here.

For much of the nineties, Chris was a young curmudgeon wearing a black Ramones jacket and Elvis Costello glasses. That's why I was surprised to see him on Freret Street, wearing a Saints hat and manning the aid line where we stood. We needed more buckets, mops, and bleach. Disaster lines were the only place to get ice in town. Chris looked surprised to see us.

"Oh, I see what side of the table we're on and what side you're on," I joked.

He gave me the worst look. "That's not even funny anymore," he said. "My family's here. I can't sit here and just watch this shit happen. I have to do something."

"They put you to work," Jake said.

"Yeah," he said, handing us a bucket to put our stuff in. "That's right . . . y'all live in Mid-City. Listen, I'm so sorry."

"Mid-Shitty," I corrected him, reminding him what he usually called it.

Before the storm, people Uptown thought Mid-City was trashy because we had Thrift City and bail bondsmen and the cheap motelville of Tulane Avenue. They'd venture over to go to Brocato's for a cannoli or to get to City Park or on their way to the Fairgrounds racetrack. Or in Chris's case probably to a show at Dixie Taverne or Rock 'n' Bowl or to watch someone's band practice in the Fountainbleau building.

"Mid-Shitty, yes," he said, finally cracking a thin smile. "If y'all need anything. I mean I don't know what I can do. Jesus. Andrew flooded, too. But anything, call me."

I had a mop and a disaster bucket filled with weird charity stuff like grape jelly pies and beard remover powder. Jake walked along bumping a full cooler of ice against his knees.

I remembered how bad I felt that we had evacuated and some of our neighbors did or could not. Chris and some of the other unfloodeds probably felt that same way plus some because their houses were dry. I hadn't really considered the lucky ducks and how they felt. There were so many bad feelings to go around, it was getting hard to keep track.

"Remind me not to joke anymore," I said.

"Yeah, you need to shut your mouth sometimes," Jake agreed.

We needed to dry out our studs, so we were doing to our house what it had done to us—bludgeoning twelve-foot horsehair plaster walls with a hammer and a cement block and watching them crumble to the floor. Small nasty gray clouds would smolder like smoke from the rubble, leaving us standing knee-deep in these piles of future work. The rubble buckets nearly pulled my arm out of its socket. I needed a dolly, but ours was flooded and rusty. After a few hours of medieval labor, Jake got the idea to bust walls onto our ruined bedclothes. Then we could each grab a side and drag the quarry comforters out the front door. Genius.

Dave was the only person we knew back in Mid-City. Ben the British musician would not be strolling his baby by on his way to the coffee shop. Paul and Helen were still in South Carolina, and Mona's was flooded; Helen would not be bopping over to bounce her toddler on the porch and chat on her way to get Middle Eastern groceries. The only diversion left in Mid-City was to stroll a wasted block to see how Dave's disaster was going.

Jake's face was strawberry red around his black rubber mask. My eyes were filled with dust. We were hot from slaving in the stinkmine and there was no running water. I took off my gloves and wiped down my arms and hands with baby wipes. I squirted a lot of antibacterial gel all over.

"Smell me," I said as we walked down the street, offering Jake my disinfected arm.

"No thanks," Jake replied. "Don't step on that wire."

"I smell like a doctor's office."

"You wish."

I knew I looked like a stranger in my filthy rubber boots with a black mask dangling around my neck, but Dave had me beat. The unholy combination of doo rag, new droopy mustache, filth, and holstered gun over his shorts had transformed him to an odd Pancho Villa.

"Wow," I said.

Jake started laughing.

"I don't want to be around an armed Dave," I said.

"Wussup?" Dave said, hugging Jake.

"The gun, Dave?" I said.

"What am I supposed to do if some nut comes rolling in here?" he said. "Holler loud and hope you hear us a block away and come save my ass? Right."

"I don't know," I answered.

"I told Marcelle's dad I would protect her. You should get one," he told Jake.

"That's what you keep saying," Jake said.

" 'Cause I'm right. Come check out my setup," he said.

We climbed his outdoor back stairs to his balcony. Earlier that summer, we had come over to get the grand tour of his new balcony deck. It had been like a treehouse nestled in the big green branches of his tree. Now the wind had blown Dave's shed's rusty tin roof into a question mark in front of his balcony, making for a conceptual view.

"Your new balcony held up great," Jake said.

"Yeah, it rocks," Dave said. "Compared to the shed."

He pointed proudly to his encampment. "Propane stove, cooler, a whole box of MREs. I have a lot of desserts left if you want 'em. Raisin nut mix? Pumpkin spice cake?"

I shook my head. So far I had managed not to eat out of any military envelopes, and I wanted to keep it that way. Also it smelled terrible at Dave's, even outside on his balcony. Like the flood, but worse. Like the water on his block had more dead stuff and underwear in it.

"Have you used these yet?" Dave said, pulling a slim packet from one of the brown MRE bags. "Watch out for these chemical heaters when you first try it. You will blow your face off. Pretty cool."

"Do these work?" Jake said, reading the back of the heater bag. "Doesn't seem like it would heat anything."

"That's what I'm saying. They get hella hot. You put some water in it then watch 'em blow. Move your face."

Dave held up a bag of dark liquid and dangled it like a magician. He grinned. "Want an iced coffee?" he asked.

"Oh my God," I said. "Where did you get that?"

Like a lot of New Orleanians, I was an iced coffee junkie. I wasn't proud of it. It gave me trouble whenever I left town and had to drink iced coffee that people claimed was just like we had in New Orleans but was actually some type of bong water that was both bitter and hot-brewed.

For years I've always had friends at this or that coffee shop in New Orleans. Buster and Clo and I could stroll around town sniffing other people's gardens and sipping free iced coffee. Iced coffee that was sweet even without sugar tasted like New Orleans to me. And Dave had it.

"Where did you get that?" Jake said again.

"It looks like an IV bag," I said.

"Cool, it kind of does. I figured out a way to make iced coffee in these cooker bags from the MREs. I used them to soak the grounds."

MREs were the ready-to-eat meals that U.S. soldiers eat. It was science and war and disaster food engineered into boxes and bags that needed no refrigeration. Dave had civilized them.

He managed two local burrito shops, so Dave was proud of his kitchen skills. I wondered if this balcony flood kitchen was his biggest culinary test yet or whether in the kitchens of New Orleans he'd seen far, far worse. He produced two go-cups and filled them from a corner of this fat envelope.

"Thanks," I said, taking a sip.

"It's been awhile," Jake said.

Dave watched us expectantly. "Pretty good, isn't it?" he said, beaming through his mustache.

"Surprisingly, yes," I said.

"Very good," Jake agreed.

"Damn right!" Dave said.

Dave leaned back against the railing of his survivor balcony, and the sun filtered through what was left of his tree. Other than the gun, curled shed roof, debris below us, and underwear of death stench, it was downright civilized. If you closed your eyes and didn't breathe in the stink too hard, it was kind of relaxing, like we'd hit REWIND and it was early August again.

"The way I look at it, is take it step by step. Have a beer, do some work, get this shit done," Dave said.

"I hope you're right," Jake said.

"I can't believe you're sleeping here," I said. "We're getting eaten alive. Aren't you getting bit?"

"I got this Deep Woods shit with extra DEET," he said. "But yeah, the mosquitoes suck. But what else am I gonna do? No one's going to get shit done who drives in from out of town every day. With all the trucks, it takes forever. You'd spend all day driving. I've got this and the restaurants to deal with. How long do you have that place Uptown for? When are those people coming back?"

"Don't know," I said.

"Then you might wind up sleeping in your upstairs," Dave said. "That's why you need one of these." He patted his gun.

Jake shook his head.

"Hope not," I said. "We have less windows left than you do. And some walls blew in."

"It's *fine*," Dave said. "Just put up some more tarp and quit your complaining. Think of your house as one giant tent."

Dave and Jake launched into a cypress siding versus HardiePlank cost-benefit analysis. I climbed down the balcony stairs. Marcelle clinked flooded dishes in the alley. She was slight with brown hair and flood dirt under her glasses. She looked more beat than Dave.

"How's it going?" I asked Marcelle.

"It's going," she said, pointing to a line of plastic tubs in which plates were soaking.

All their wedding china sat soaking in bleach in these tubs in the sun. They had recently gotten married. I had thrown out every last pot and dish in my kitchen and felt wasteful about doing it.

"I threw it all out. Almost everything. Even the stuff above the waterline. The steam even was filth," I said. "I read some disaster pamphlet that said all wood and plastic have to go. Some glass you can bleach. Nothing with cracks, blah, blah, blah. There's like this whole long list."

"Yeah," she said.

Watching Marcelle stoop and frown and stir her bleach tubs with a spoon, I was glad I was not a newlywed with feelings spread all over some china plates. I also felt kind of embarrassed. I'd known Marcelle for a few years, but not all that well. We had only watched some bands together and laughed. Now all her best things were out on the sidewalk and Jake and I were tromping through. I made a mental note—if I'm ever invited for dinner, don't eat off any china.

A few days after power was restored Uptown, my friend sent a partier and a DJ with an afro to move in with the dogs and us. The storm had knocked off the electricity to their Creole cottage in the Treme. Soon after, my friend called again to say another lady was moving in for a few days. Could we let her in?

Soon a neat, smartly-dressed older black woman arrived. She had lived in Gentilly and was back to try to salvage what she could from her second-story apartment. She looked way too clean for what I knew awaited her. I showed her where we kept our latex gloves and N-95 masks if she needed them.

The Gentilly woman had been stuck with her dogs in a stranger's house near Lafayette since the storm. She did not know how or if she could ever move back. Since she had been renting in Gentilly, she was now homeless. She had to figure out how to get her hands on an apartment somewhere where she did not have a life. And one that would allow pets.

The house was now filled with rattled people. We started taking Buster and Clo to Mid-City with us most days so they would not get on anyone's frayed nerves. The dogs hated it at our house now.

They seemed pitifully confused as to why we would not stop treating them so terribly. They were banned from their own backyard. It was filled with our collapsing fence and shed and parts of other people's houses. Downstairs was also off limits. It was too contaminated for sniffing. Jake would carry Clo and then Buster all the way from the backseat of the car to upstairs so their feet did not get cut. Over our hammering, busting, and dragging, we could hear them baying all day.

One afternoon I came back to my friend's house beat from

cursing and beating our walls all day. The older woman was back from packing early, having tea at the kitchen table. I turned on the sink to scrub the day's filth from my arms.

"How'd it go?" I said.

"I'm getting it done," she replied. "Though I'm not sure for what. The lady who's been letting me stay with her has been nice, very nice. I'm not saying that. But what am I going to do? I've lived my whole life in New Orleans. I'm not old, but I'm not young. I can't be staying out there."

I wasn't sure what to say. There were no answers. "The whole thing's terrible," I agreed. "Maybe some people will get stuff fixed quick."

"Maybe, maybe not. Then they say the rent is going to go through the roof." She gazed wistfully at me and my mess at the sink.

"I know you don't feel lucky now," she said. "But I just wish I had something to *fix*."

Chapter 7

pit bull jesus

I did not want to lose my pit bull Jesus. He was three feet tall and solid clay. Pit bull Jesus was bright brown with dreadlocks and regal in flowing coral and island blue robes. He was a handmade, DIY Jesus—better than the cool alabaster savior I had grown up with at Holy Ghost.

Pit bull Jesus had open arms outstretched as if in blessing, but actually he was waiting for someone to hand him a pit bull on a leash. The pit bull was the part of this statue that the middle schooler talked up a lot but never got around to finishing before forsaking Jesus completely. Before the kid's teacher junked Jesus with the rest of the year's discarded ideas, she gave him to me. I finished the statue as best I could and added some stigmata and fired him in a kiln. And so I had come to foster pit bull Jesus. He had ruled the earthly corner in front of my bookshelves until the day the water came.

I liked pit bull Jesus. Like a Japanese magnolia tree pinkening in spring or the I-Have-Oranges-and-Banana-Man singing his fruit song from blocks away, pit bull Jesus bestowed many holy mysteries—like how did a child sculpt a face so calm and perfect and why does the Prince of Peace require a fighting breed? He had been totally inundated in my murky house for weeks but, wonder of wonders, had only a few broken dreads.

Now I wanted him gone before I caused him any further harm.

Jake and I each grabbed an outstretched arm and lugged him outside away from our swinging hammers and falling plaster and into the neighbor's Virgin Mary grotto directly across the street.

I leaned him in close to Mary. "How does he look?" I asked.

"Good. But someone's going to steal him and you're going to be mad," Jake said.

"People don't do that," I said. "That's like a sin. Mary's been out here for years. Probably decades. No one's messed with her."

"Mary's cement. You'd need a forklift to steal Mary."

"You can't melt him down like copper plumbing," I said. "Who's going to steal him?"

"Somebody," Jake said. "Some hippie."

"They better not. They're not coming back. The party's over."

"Wait and see," Jake muttered.

"Stolen's better than broken," I continued. "I don't want anything anymore. I can't stand to see one more thing get ruined. I don't want to be responsible for anything."

One of those mirrored-sunglasses, mustached guys in an orange vest stopped poking at the crooked power lines with his pole and started smirking toward me. I spooned into my barbecue veggie burger MRE envelope and ignored him. I knew I looked plaster-dusted and ridiculous sitting on a garbage bag on my steps. I knew I had a surgical mask hanging around my neck. And since I'd heard they were getting overtime to hang out in the hellhole and I wasn't, I felt it was rude of him to be laughing.

Above all, I did not care to hear anything he had to say. A few days earlier, an orange-vester had sidled up to try to comfort me. "You know what Katrina means? It means *cleansing*," he had said. "I think in the long run all of y'all are going to wind up a *lot* better off. The undesirables are going to stay washed away."

Sure, who wouldn't want all the undesirables washed away? Problem was, I doubted his undesirables and mine were the same. In fact, I was probably one of his undesirables. Also, in the non-scriptural world, here in reality, the word *cleansing* had ominous ethnic undertones. I had spent the majority of my life in a majority-black city, much of it in a majority-black neighborhood. As far as I could tell, none of us were waiting for God to send a storm to wash the other away.

He was not the first disaster guy to look at my work gloves and work boots and baseball cap and white face and decide I was someone I wasn't. Since my fence was down, another disaster man with a clipboard had waltzed into my backyard to ask me some question. He brought up the rumored coming influx of Hispanic laborers. "I don't see what everyone's getting all up in arms about the Mexicans coming. As far as I'm concerned," he said, "we need some new niggers around here anyway."

I'm not naive, but still I was shocked. Maybe because I had removed myself from the Other South environment, I had not had anyone speak this way to me since I was a kid. It had made me sad and nervous to hear it then, especially when out of the mouth of a relative or a friend's dad. Mom had taught us that racism was wrong. When she was a girl and would have to leave the Hungarian Settlement to go to town, she never enjoyed being called a *hunkie* by the rural Louisiana kids.

On the settlement, Mom spent many seasons in the field picking strawberries and playing with migrant workers' children. I could not begin to understand what had gone on in the forties between the poor Hungarian Americans with a small piece of land and some of the poorer African American migrant workers with no piece of land. But when I was a child, I had peeked in the door of the empty "picker sheds" with their rickety bunks ten yards from Mom's own childhood bed. Those buildings scared me. Something I saw on television on *Roots* looked suspiciously like the picker sheds. Mom tried to explain how they weren't the same. But just like she could never quite clarify my childish questions about the caveman-cowboy timeline, I never quite believed her.

Grown men around my small town were often racist, what Mom called *ignorant*. This made adults in general seem suspect to me. Being stuck in my ruined New Orleans garden with broken men who were supposed to be in charge made me feel trapped all over again.

There is something about a woman alone in a rubblescape. Before I could finish my barbecue veggie disaster burger, this latest orange-vester could no longer resist. "I'm guessing you've never been in the military," he called over my busted picket fence.

"Nope," I said.

He grinned. "That's what I figured. Well, I hope you haven't been chewing that gum then."

"Why?" I asked. Jake had.

"You know that's a laxative."

I made a face. I wondered what else was wrong with these things. MREs were free and you did not have to drive outside the city limits to an open grocery store to get them.

"I'm sick of eating peanut butter sandwiches with latex gloves," I said.

"I bet you are," he said. "Just thought you'd want to know."

"Thanks," I said.

I dumped the rest of my MRE food envelopes out of my box on the porch and started reading the fine print. *Partially hydrogenated* this; *partially hydrogenated* that. What the hell. Giving any benefit of the doubt whatsoever in regards to the government was becoming dangerous.

In the past, I had been told to keep a hatchet in the attic "just in case" I needed to hack my way onto the roof. And I had dismissed this as a stupid old Louisiana wives' tale. Turns out not. Now I realized hatchet attics were great and only an idiot would think it was a good idea to eat anything that could be dropped by parachute.

I went to find Jake. He was sorting through some flooded, wadded papers on the back porch. I wanted that part over with already. I wished he would just throw it all away.

"Jake, no more MREs," I said. "They're full of laxatives and transfat."

"What?"

"Well, they might be full of laxative, but they're definitely full of transfat."

"You're kidding," he said. "Yuck."

I held out a khaki envelope for proof. "Read this," I said.

"Nah," he said. "I take your word for it."

"Where's our old hand ax?" I said. "In the pile of rusty tools you won't throw out?"

"Probably."

"I'm sticking it in the attic."

"Okay," he said, giving me a funny look.

"Want to hear something weird?"

"Not particularly. I'm going through these. *Sucks.*"

A pile of dried, brown mortgage and insurance papers stuck together in a wad in a mildewed folder. He frowned and tried to shake the pages apart while wearing thick, orange chemical gloves.

"Throw that out. It's disgusting," I said. "Get them to send them to us again."

"The insurance won't call me back," he said. "We need these."

"Then let's get a Ziploc or something. Those are going to make you sick."

He threw down his folderwad in disgust on the back porch. He had been attempting to flatten a line of curled photos by pinning their edges under chunks of plaster. Jake as a tan child at a lake summer camp. Jake as a cowboy with a pony named Teddy-bear. Jake as a bangs-in-the-eyes skater kid. Jake and some other twenty-something band guys goosing each other on a sidewalk after a show. All the Jakes were drying into smears in the sun.

"Some of those look okay," I said.

"No they don't," he replied.

"Want to hear my paranoid thought?"

"I don't know. Do I?"

"You know how the canal walls failed and the levees failed?" I asked.

"Yeah."

"Well then, why are we supposed to think that the Mississippi River levees supposedly maintained by the same nutjobs are for some reason miraculously made right?"

"Good question," Jake said.

"You don't think that's PTSD talking?" I said.

Some people said we were all going to get PTSD. I liked to point out possible instances of it to myself occasionally in hopes that would stave it off. But some things that seemed squirrelly on the surface, like the hatchet, also seemed like common sense. Which is I guess how men wind up wearing aluminum foil hats.

"Maybe PTSD," Jake said. "But it's true."

"Then why does everyone Uptown not worry about that?" I said. "Like, eew, sucks to be you but I'm sleeping all comfy in the sliver by the river."

"No clue," he said. "Less PTSD? Denial?"

"Well they better get their hatchets ready is all I'm saying. I don't know if we should fix the house," I said. "Even if other people do."

"I know," he said.

I was grateful for Uptown. You could drive for over half an hour across the city and not see anything that slightly resembled what

it had been. But Uptown and the French Quarter was New Orleans reduced to its thin, historical core. The whole city couldn't
cram into it, but it was still living proof of the New Orleans the
national news claimed was gone without a trace.

When the power returned Uptown, someone's Web server
buzzed back on in a closed coffee shop. Civilization seemed on the
horizon. I would spend all day in the Stone Age of Mid-City where
we still had to truck in water, but Uptown I could sit cross-legged
on the sidewalk with modern humans and check e-mail.

But even in the good parts of town, the spared parts, weird-
ness prevailed. Along the broken streetcar tracks on St. Charles
we had watched a woman with a facelift and a horse promenade.
It was as if she had waited a lifetime for the streetcar to go offline
so she could parade. In the Garden District, Jake and I went to
check on Tanio's dad. We covered our faces and ran through the
darkest cloud of driveway flies we had seen yet, a two-refrigerator
nest, and found him standing alone outside his ballroom, clutching a beer and staring into his blackened backyard pool.

The sudden depopulation of the city and the invasion by disaster contractors from that Other South unnerved me. They
weren't just in my yard. They were all over. Walking the dogs, I
heard country music blaring from jacked-up trucks rolling down
Magazine Street. It wasn't the New Orleans I knew.

Stopped, revving at a traffic-light with me and Buster and Clo
on the sidewalk beside them, an occasional truck guy would call
out, "You hunt them dogs?"

"Just crawfish and food on the street," I'd say.

It was my standard answer, and it wasn't that funny. But around
New Orleans it usually elicited a cry of "the good stuff!" or a head
shake or a chuckle. But from the disaster truck men, blank stares
or, worse yet, "That's a shame."

There was something chilling about driving into New Orleans
and hearing Public Radio Mississippi or "new country" blaring

on the radio. A life without WTUL college radio odd-rock, a life without jazz and brass bands on WWOZ, a life without hearing a very old woman read what cuts of sirloin were on sale on Radio for the Blind was not the life for me.

Weirdest was the new quiet. In pre-Katrina New Orleans, children often walked down the street practicing marching band instruments. Friends' bands played. Neighbor kids blasted Q-93. To return to my neighborhood to find children and music washed away was spooky. If we were going to consider fixing our house, I needed to believe not only that I would not drown in my bed, but also that the days of disaster information broadcasts and contractors in pickup trucks blasting "song, song of the south, sweet potato pie and shut my mouth" would soon end.

Directly across the street, the Dupres' mustard-colored shotgun house with the Mary grotto looked pristine even after the flood. If you squinted you could not see the faint flood scum line. The grotto flowers had drowned, but Mary stood strong and now had a brightly painted son to keep her company.

The Dupre couple were well into their eighties and had never called the cops on Jake's band practices as long as the band knocked off at a reasonable time. Mr. Dupre wore suspenders and a smart golf cap. When the Dupres would leave the house, he would back his car from the back of their long driveway to the front steps so that Mrs. Dupre could have door-to-door service. During the years we had the wife beater—and the screams—next door to us, across the street, Jake would spy a face (above Mary), obscured by lace curtain, peeking. Though we had all kept mostly to ourselves, nodding "hi" and "bye" and saying "hot enough for ya?" and waving, Mrs. Dupre was one of the block grandmothers; she had once given one of our friends a nice dress shirt. She spoke with the comforting, familiar, somewhat-Brooklyn-sounding New Orleans accent that some of my older relatives have.

One day I came outside and Mrs. Dupre had reappeared on our decimated street, hand over her mouth. Her adult daughter was holding her up by the elbows as they ventured inside her flooded house. In their idling car, Mr. Dupre sat white as a ghost in the backseat.

I had already seen the sixty-something sisters return to their huge, white double-camelback next door to her, so I knew the language of hands on faces. The first time people came back to their houses after the flood, they usually walked around hushed as if at a wake. But sometimes the viewing escalated to throwing of buckets and yelling—like the day these two chubby men in their fifties had almost come to blows.

I was tossing out bleach water. Mrs. Dupre stepped back onto her porch alone and spotted me. She waved me over. I took off my gloves and crossed the street.

"I'm glad my mother is not alive to see this," she said. "I want you to know that all my life is in there. My whole life. Nice stuff. Good stuff. We had all-wood cabinets. Cherry."

"I'm so sorry," I said.

"We've been living by my daughter's because you know my husband is so sick, honey, he got the Alzheimer's."

"No, I hadn't heard that. So sorry," I said again.

"You and me both. I hope this doesn't kill him."

Jake walked across the street to join us. He held out a mask. "Need a mask?" he asked.

"Thank you, honey, but we don't have any mold. Not much," she said. "This is an old house. Look how good it stood. Plaster."

I peeked inside. It was all carpet in there. No way she didn't have mold. But a lot of people liked to say they didn't have mold. She wasn't the first to say it to me.

"We'll be around some trying to clean up. We'll keep an eye out for you," I said.

"Oh, would you? I would feel so much better. Do not let anybody, I mean *anybody* go in my house. My whole life is in there. I mean, I know you can't stop them. But you know what I mean. Keep an eye out.

"Come say hello to my husband," she said. "He has been feeling terrible. He can't go in there. He does not need to see this."

She pointed to our old neighbor pale in the backseat.

"Hello, Mr. Dupre, remember me?" Jake said.

Mr. Dupre nodded tentatively.

"It's the nice boy who bought the house across the street," his wife said, leaning over into the car. "He and his wife are going to watch the house for us. Nothing to worry about."

"Right," she stage-whispered, making a face at me.

That's when she spotted pit bull Jesus shining brown, blue and coral, snuggled up next to her flooded Mary.

"Will you look at this. It came in on the water. I like it. It's God telling us something. What is he telling us, do you think?" she asked me.

I had always thought of him as saying, "Hey, where's my pit bull?" But now I wasn't so sure.

"That Mary's watching over New Orleans?" Mrs. Dupre said. "That black and white people should all try to get along?"

"I don't know," I said. "Maybe."

"This? I'm leaving this. Now this is something else," Mrs. Dupre suddenly chuckled. "It's a hurricane miracle."

backyard glider

My croissant was crunchy brown and chewy with buttery layers like hope. It tasted like New Orleans before the flood and the French Resistance. The croissant helped me forget that I was dressed for misery. I was sitting at an outdoor café table wearing a men's undershirt that came in a pack, my ruined red Mary Janes, and some humanitarian teen's Abercrombie & Fitch cargo pants. I had fished them out of a disaster-line charity box. In an effort to feel normal, I refused to step into my disaster boots until we got to Mid-City.

The French family was baking fast and furious to help feed those of us who were back. Since we had been eating junk for weeks, I wanted to kiss their French feet. We were on our way to our house to work, but first we were going to the Quarter to throw out a spoiled refrigerator for an elderly lady. Jake had abandoned his croissant to answer his cell phone. When he returned a few minutes later, he grinned.

"Did you take a bite of my croissant?" Jake said.

"Why would I do that?"

"You tell me," Jake said, sitting down. "That was the insurance."

"You're kidding."

Jake had been calling the insurance company almost every day. At first he spoke Southern and polite to everyone, "sir"ing and "ma'am"ing all the phone agents like a child, like if he followed the rules of his upbringing strictly enough everything would fall into place. But that soon changed. Sometimes when I walked outside, I found Jake standing between our garbage pile and his flooded van yelling. *I'm standing on my street right now, so I know it's not true that you can't get here. There's no more water. I'm standing here RIGHT NOW on dirt! Dry dirt! It's dusty! I drove a car here.*

We still did not know what to do about the house or ourselves. We were stuck without hearing from the insurance company. Our pre–Hurricane Rita tarp job wasn't cutting it. We had since reinforced it, lashing the ends of the tarp to the porch columns. But even though we had nailed, tacked, and tied it, our tarp job still puffed like a bright blue sail in the breeze. Even if we could not fix the house, we wanted to at least get a new roof. In theory, a gutted house with a new roof would be worth more than a Petri dish if we had to sell it.

In the newspaper FEMA told everyone *Operation Blue Roof is coming! Operation Blue Roof is coming!* And with real tarp technology. So Jake called the number. So far Operation Blue Roof *wasn't* coming. Not to us or any other houses I'd seen in Mid-City. Maybe they would, but I didn't really believe it.

Recently, the insurance people had called and finally agreed to meet. Jake had been relieved. He had run up and down our new sublet in his socks, giddier than I'd seen him in months, sliding on the polished wood floors with Clo and Buster barking and spinning at his feet. On the day of our appointment, we waited and waited in rubbleville. They never came. It felt like being left at the altar. Moving on to the next stage in this trial, detecting any progress or forward motion at all had quickly become that big a deal.

Jake popped the last of his croissant into his mouth.

"Guess what the insurance wanted?" Jake said.

"They claim they're coming again," I said.

"Nope," Jake said. "That was it."

"They're not coming? They're not going to even try?"

"No, that was *it* it. That was it."

"That was *it*? How could that be it? They did it on the phone?"

"Yup."

"Then why wouldn't they do it on the phone over a month ago?"

"I don't know. They just did," he said. "I yelled instead of acting nice."

We were trying to figure out best flood practices. A few people had counseled Jake to pour on the sugar. But some other guys had told him to survive this he needed to man-up considerably and learn to be a dick. It was all a bunch of Dale Carnegie disaster bull really. On the other hand, we were blasted open and would try anything. It was the world's biggest teachable moment.

"Let me get this straight," I said. "Because you yelled, they did it on the phone."

"Possibly. Or it's just utterly random depending on their mood or who answers the phone. Hard to tell. But that's it for the flood part. We still have to meet with the wind guy, but that's it for that."

He wrote a number on a napkin and slid it over.

It was a number. It was something; it was nothing. It looked like gibberish. It was more money than either of us had ever had at one time but still not enough. To fix all that was wrong with the house or buy a new one in New Orleans would cost more. Not that there were many people left in New Orleans to hire anyway. I felt encouraged and discouraged. I was not used to turning what I thought was a corner only to have the corner recede.

"What if we just took that money and said screw it and went to Europe for a year?" I mused.

"Or Costa Rica for three," Jake said.

A guy Jake knew had surfed Costa Rica. Since then Jake sometimes got this beach look in his eye and brought up Costa Rica. Once I bought him a surfboard from someone's yard sale in

Mid-City. Instead of Costa Rica, Jake said he was going to bring it to down the Louisiana coast to Grand Isle. But then someone stole his car with the board in it from in front of our house.

"Or Vietnam for however long," I said.

Before the storm, some Vietnamese families that lived near my friend's house in New Orleans East had these amazing rice paddies in their backyard canals. I had heard that in Vietnam the green water gardens stretched like that for miles.

"Vietnam would be awesome," Jake said. "But not happening."

He ripped up the napkin with the number on it and handed me the pieces.

"That's what they're giving to the mortgage company."

Helen's sandy blond cut was tousled. A rubber mold mask hung from her neck. She put her hand on my arm in front of her ruined house.

"Oh, *Cheryl,* aren't you *scared*?" Helen asked.

"Scared how?" I said. "Some days it's not as deserted. There are a few more people coming to get their things. Mostly it's just depressing."

Actually I was scared. Our work outlook was still sketchy, so I was scared of going broke. I was also scared of having to jump into a snuffing, fifty-hour-a-week job somewhere I never wanted to be. I was scared of being homeless. Our new sublet was very temporary.

Most bizarrely, I was actually also scared of drowning. I was a good swimmer but sometimes at night when I was trying to fall asleep I found myself thinking weird stuff, like about dog life preservers and if we should get a hard plastic kayak to keep in the attic. These were thoughts I chose to ignore, aluminum foil hat thoughts, assuming they would go away. These thoughts would get worse when neighbors returned and told me their flood stories.

A bald neighbor with a dangling crucifix earring came back to salvage his stuff. He was wild eyed in a way he had not been before. He was talking loud and waving his arms.

"Did you see me on CNN? I had to swim to Hollygrove to get a boat to take people off their porch. I had to pull a fence board for a paddle. When we got to the interstate, when they finally came to get us, they put a gun in my face. I said, I know that must be a camera. I said I *know* you must be taking my picture now because I know that ain't no gun in my face. Luckily I was medical. Luckily I had a cut getting infected or we never would have got off that interstate to the airport at *all*."

When he saw me dusty from gutting walls instead of doing what he and his wife had come to do—salvaging what they could and leaving—he shook his head.

"Oh, nah. You're not staying, are you? I'll tell you one thing. They pumped that water in. It was the next day. The sun was shining. That storm was *over* when that water start coming up the street. Then it came a little higher, a little higher, up to the porch. I told my kids wake me up when it gets in the house. They *pumped* that water in. Had to."

Who wouldn't be rattled some days? But I didn't feel like telling Helen all that. She had enough on her plate.

"Not scared of *people*," she said, in her sweet, Helen singsong voice. "Of *mold*. Of *toxins*. Paul thinks there might really be some really *bad toxins* we don't know about. *Mold* and there was that *oil* spill. I hate to leave our little house, but we don't want the baby here in all of that."

"That Murphy spill was all the way in Chalmette," I said. "But y'all are right. No way you should have him in Mid-City right now. But there might be some children back Uptown."

"But the toxins could have all floated around. Paul thinks there could be contamination *everywhere*. And *lead*."

"There was lead before," I said. "Plenty. I'm not drinking any-

thing out of the taps. They say it's okay Uptown, but I'm not drinking it. They also say there's thousands of breaks in the waterlines.
So which is it? I'm trying to take just like a quick shower."

Helen giggled. She had a very fine, full-body giggle that punc-
tured the wind out of any given situation.

"Oh, *Cheryl*. You're trying to take a quick shower. It's not
funny," she giggled. "Can you believe this?"

"No," I said.

"Come see my new floor. Remember we just got it refinished?"
Helen said. "It's a *wreck*. I don't know how I'm ever going to go
through all my stuff. We decided it's time to start simplifying."

I felt bad for Helen. My writing projects had been on my laptop. There was no way all her film stuff could have fit with her,
the baby, Paul, and Rosie the pig in their evacuation car. And that
summer she had said she was up against a big deadline. How to
keep your That's-a-Great-Idea life going without letting drudgery life interfere was a problem we had often discussed. But now
Helen on my porch chatting about her film seemed like an eon
ago. The ultimate drudgery life that was the flood had arrived.

Jake and Paul came around the corner from Paul and Helen's
backyard.

"I'm going to give Paul Tim's number," Jake said. "He might
need someone to gut."

Paul looked a little tired, but good in his mold mask, like haz-
ard gear was just another snazzy Paul ensemble.

"Cheryl, Jake said you already took your walls out?" Paul said.

"A lot of them downstairs," I said. "To begin to treat and
dry the studs before the mold really got going. We went to this
seminar."

Helen sighed. "I just hate throwing everything away," she said.

"You don't have to throw that out," I told Helen, pointing to
her three-seater metal glider. It was a sturdy, and cream and sage
instead of rusted through like most New Orleans porch furniture.

"I saved some like it. You bleach it and hose it and scrub it and spray this stuff on it to stop the rust."

"Oh really? That's so great," Helen said. "Oh, we can't move it. How about you take it? That way I'll come glide on it in your yard when I get back!"

I liked the way Helen thought. I looked at Jake. He shrugged.

"Deal," I said.

I felt like throwing myself at Helen's feet and saying, "Don't go!" It wasn't that we were best friends or even everyday friends. We were just friends. But I didn't want to get cancer from the toxins like Paul said. And I did not want to be left alone in Mid-City.

It was sad watching friend after friend leave. A British musician friend, Ben, two houses down from us, a sixties Psychedelia buff, lost years of collectible records. His grandfather's baby grand, recently shipped from England, stewed in his swampish living room. Watching him sitting on his flooded bathroom floor stirring dozens of CDs in a bathtub full of bleach, I felt like someone should apologize for American engineering. Jake helped him wrestle a rug that had swelled to hundreds of waterlogged pounds on a flat dolly down his front steps instead. Soon after, Ben left with his wife and her job for good. He would not be lugging Jake's Rhodes piano down the street ever again.

When Jake told Ben that he was considering fixing the house, Ben looked at Jake like he had gone native. Looking around Mid-City months after the flood, a few things were clear. If no one attempted to fix any of the old houses in any of our old neighborhoods, house by house, block by block, our New Orleans would be lost.

The van had flooded. So I picked up one end of Helen and Paul's backyard glider and Jake picked up the other.

"Ready?" I said.

"Got it," Jake said.

I liked the idea of shining the glider up and keeping in my backyard a place for Helen to sit. It made me feel like my garden was on its way back. But after three blocks of baby steps around flooded cars and ruin, I felt tired and stupid. Like when you're in college and put a mattress on top of someone's tiny car and suddenly you're the jerk hanging out the window holding on for dear life with one hand on the mattress. All of a sudden I saw what Ben saw—two people who had maybe gone flood crazy. I dropped my end.

"Why are we doing this?" I said.

"You're the one who wanted it," Jake said.

"You wanted it, too," I said.

"I didn't want it or not want it," Jake said.

"That's not true," I said. "I can't believe you would say that. You're just saying that now because you don't want to carry it!"

Jake sighed. He ran a latex-gloved hand through his hair. I hoped it was not just me who had stuck him here in the middle of this lonesome plaster-dusted street.

"I don't *mind* carrying it," he finally said. "But it's almost impossible with you talking and dropping your part every few feet. I'm willing to carry it. But you're going to have to try harder on your end."

I hoisted the glider.

"Okay," I said.

plenty enough suck to go around

Clo climbed up in the poet's puffy chair.

"Come check out Madam Robichaux," I called to Jake.

"Hold on. I'm trying to leave another message for this electrician," Jake said.

When she wasn't lolling on the upstairs porch with Buster, Clo sat completely vertical on her flat basset tush in the poet's thinking chair. She gazed out the window. It was exactly how I imagined the poet himself did it when he was in town.

I yelled across the sublet.

"I already called every A-to-H electrician in the phone book. A lot of the numbers don't work. Let's give it a rest for today."

"One minute," Jake yelled back.

Normal things weren't working right. It seemed like we better get used to it. Stoplights all over town were shattered and leaning. People were zooming the opposite way down one-way streets. Because the majority of the city had flooded, the old Yellow Pages didn't work either.

We had decided to tell the mortgage company we would be our own contractors. So far Jake and Cheryl Bros. Construction had surveyed our shoddy levees and ghost town of a neighborhood and determined we were only fixing the roof and the wiring. But we were having a labor problem. Practically no one but a Louisiana Himalaya Association, friend-of-a-friend architect would call us back—and possibly him only because it was part of his spiritual practice.

But other things were looking up. Jake and Cheryl Bros. now had a landline instead of just pay-by-minute cell phones. We had scored an affordable, dog-friendly sublet. The apartment was a sweet, sweet resort on the Isle of Denial Uptown. It had things Jake and I didn't have before the flood—a dishwasher, central air, and an upstairs porch. A downstairs neighbor had even power-washed the sidewalks. It was the apartment of a video editor friend and his boyfriend the poet. They were trying Austin on for size until New Orleans got less woolly. Though they were a perfectly urban New Orleans couple, I pictured them tossing back frozen margaritas over in Texas and boot-scooting barefoot in cowboy hats.

All the moving and incarceration had set the dogs' teeth on edge. Clo had taken to nipping at Buster occasionally to seize what little turf was left. But in this new sublet they looked more like the spoiled dogs they were instead of the raggedy detainees they had become going with us to Mid-City every day. Here Clo could sit in a puffy chair, and I could imagine that the shelves of books were my new replacement library.

Jake walked in scowling.

"What are we going to do if no electricians will come give us an estimate?" Jake said.

"We already got one," I reminded him.

Jake shook his head in disgust. "I will burn the house down before I will ever, ever give some douche bag twenty-two thousand dollars for a simple rewiring," he said.

"I know," I said. "I'm with you. But check out Clo in her thinking chair. She's lording the manor thinking up a sonnet."

Jake almost smiled. "Pretty relaxed," he agreed.

"Maybe you should try and get your mind off it some when we're not in the hellhole," I said.

"I know," Jake said. "But I want this shit over with."

After a day of sweating filth and manning the front yard di-saster confessional, I could now barely wait to drive back to un-flooded New Orleans and shut the door. In Mid-City, neighbors I barely knew turned up every few days to sort and toss their lives, needing latex gloves, a spare mold mask, or to unburden. I lis-tened to their stories about the four dogs they loved and drowned and the parrot they let go the night of the storm. I listened to how there were ten relatives living piled up at someone's mom's house. I heard my mouth say a lot of words that needed to be said that I wasn't sure were true. *There's nothing else you could have done* and *You did the best you could* and *I can look at you and tell you're the kind of person who is going to be okay.*

I wasn't religious, or even necessarily Catholic anymore, more guilty agnostic. But I would look across the street at Mary and her dreadlocked son in the flood grotto and think, Lord help me, pit bull Jesus. Then I would go back Uptown.

Uptown I could wash off the disaster dirt in the tub with Clo snoring on the bathmat next to me. I could pretend that we would not soon be out on our butts again. I could have a tiny speck of my old New Orleans life back. As soon as we took out their moldy fridge and helped haul in the new one, I bought milk and put some coffee on to soak.

A few weeks into this sublet we got lucky enough to enjoy hot water again, which a lot of people in unflooded New Orleans still did not have. In a random switch of events, I was suddenly not a charity boarder crammed with Jake and the dogs sniffing mold in someone's back room. I was the hostess with the mostest. I e-mailed a friend without hot water and told her she should come over and stop taking her whore's bath in her sink.

But everyone could not see I had climbed halfway back up to the top of my world. People's emotions were brimming and slop-ping all over. One day I was walking Clo and Buster Uptown, and they stopped to sniff a businessman's two fluffy dogs. I remarked how green and beautiful it was away from the garbage piles and flood mess of our neighborhood. There were still *trees*. "I really admire what you people are doing," the man in the suit said, tears springing to his eyes. For a second I was afraid he was going to give me ten dollars or hug me. Or start weeping in earnest. I knew he shouldn't be crying for me, but, then again, he probably wasn't.

Our new sublet was so reputable, I wanted Mom to come back and see us again. Her first visit had not gone well. She had pulled up next to the stinking garbage piles lining our block and Jake's dead van. She had stepped out of her car in front of my house sobbing. She had scolded me for not warning her. "You didn't tell me it would look . . . so . . . *bad*."

I had not sugarcoated anything. The only vaguely positive news I had reported back was that old houses were strong and fixable—that, amazingly, water drains right out the cracks between the floorboards and drips past the masonry piers three feet to the ground below. I had said that her old church, St. Joseph, on Tulane Avenue, was intact and so were our family graves. Not a particularly rosy picture.

She had rubbed her eyes with the back of her hand like a little girl and leaned against my broken porch.

"All those *cars*," she said.

"I know," I said.

The dozens of milky cars still lining the neutral ground and curbs months after the flood looked like a bunch of beached whales trying to save themselves. Suffering that is so immense, so woeful in its scale, I probably didn't properly warn her of that. It looked like the absence of hope. What were you supposed to say? Maybe a person had to be able to grip tightly in her mind a vision of the opposite in order to manage the sight of it. Mom's was slipping.

"Your garden," she cried.

My garden reminded Mom of when she lived Uptown with her aunt; Aunt Mary had a front-yard rose garden and bell peppers growing in the back. Mom had ferried a lot of plants from her yard down to me in New Orleans to green my own garden over the years. In return, I had sent irises, magnolia fuscata, and some scrambling yellow roses Mom's way. And my aunt out near the settlement sent me daylilies. After a girlhood spent farming, in her older years mom's sister had gone ornamental crazy. Near a shed of barking beagles, she had several blooming acres of daylilies in hundreds of rainbow species.

True, some of them drowned in my yard. But, in another sense, so what? The yard had been nothing in the mid-nineties. The backyard was rocks and crazy grass and dirt mixed with a hundred years of oyster shells. There was a terminally diseased plum tree. Candy wrappers, stamp-sized Ziploc drug bags, and an occasional condom littered the front. I might not *feel* like reseeding, but I knew I could. I had seen it bloom to life once already.

I kicked a dusty new octopus with my foot. It had been a huge succulent. After the flood, it had collapsed to a heap.

"Look at the century plant Jake's stepdad Jack brought me from Florida," I said. "Kind of neat like that."

"Gross," Mom said. "Gross, gross, gross."

I didn't only see it like that. Sometimes I tried to picture what my yard had looked like underwater. In the less murky version it was not the pit bull puppy that had paddled up to my friend's dad's canoe. It was a sea garden with sea sprite ladies in old Nola housecoats tumbling on bright strawberry bottlebrush tree anemones. In the sea garden, old century plants were blue squids. A filthy Barbie backstroked by.

But before Mom came again I needed to recharge. I had a book friend whose car had been smoked to barbecue during the storm in the Canal Place fire. Her apartment had flooded a few insidious inches. She still had a job but was living on someone's futon and beginning one of those post-storm breakups that were going around like the flu. I called to tell her we had real wineglasses, both kinds. Would she care to join us for a three-course disaster food-stamp dinner? We would talk not about mold or who lost what and was scrambling to get it back. No one would mention whose family had really abandoned them in the aftermath but only something shimmering someone once had the time to read. She thought that was a great idea.

As unflooded people trickled back to stay, Jake and I would over-hear them at the drugstore bitterly complaining. They hated the curfew. They were upset about their manicurist being displaced, their favorite restaurant not reopening, and all the stores still be-ing closed. They had to drive all the way out to Jefferson Parish to replace a broken gate lock. "Can you believe?" they said.

There was a trite mantra I found myself having to say out loud to myself—everyone's loss is big to them—to keep from hating people. It would happen time and again. Sometimes Jake would say it to me. Sometimes I would say it to him.

People were shuddering across the flooded neighborhoods. Returning to the sublet in unflooded New Orleans, we would hear troubles like "They're going to stay at their vacation house for a while until things settle down" and "Her parents simply in-sisted she transfer to NYU." Jake would roll his eyes. We would exchange glances. A particularly puffy complaint might elicit an involuntary exhalation from Jake, like he had been punched in the stomach. "Come the fuck on," he would mutter.

To which I would sometimes bite my lip and say, whether I believed it at that second or not, "Everyone's loss is big and scary to them."

"Right," Jake would say.

"Yeah," I'd agree, and put it away to take out another time.

But I took it out a lot. I could feel a small, bad person willing to be born growing somewhere inside me. I didn't want to meet her.

The weird thing was that this little bon mot of trite was actually true. People had lost their faith. Our city was in ruin. That's why businessmen in fine suits walking fluffy white dogs could break down. People in perfectly dry houses found themselves drinking a suddenly sour mimosa. I was not interested in sifting and weighing suck on a bunch of tiny scales. Suck was too hard to quantify. There was plenty enough suck to go around. Sitting around measuring it wasn't going to fix anything.

Flooded people started to grumble that unflooded people were *spoiled*. And some days I was one of them. But in my unbitter, unflooded heart I didn't believe people should be happy they had just lost their jobs or all their life plans. If unflooded people were spoiled for being rattled that their city and security had been shredded around them, then I should be thrilled that "at least I had an upstairs." And I really was. But I also wasn't.

perfectly simple solutions

I was prying long pieces of lath from the cypress wall studs when I heard Jake scream. I rushed out in the backyard. Jake was holding one leg like a flamingo with his fist in his mouth. A board from the collapsing shed was attached to the bottom of his foot like a propeller.

"Jesus," Jake whimpered.

"Let me see," I said, trying not to smile.

"Help me get this out," Jake said. "Stop laughing."

"I'm not laughing," I said, smiling like a fiend. "Sorry."

I have taken First Aid and can and will help in a medical emergency, but if a person is in a certain amount of pain, I am also going to laugh. I am not laughing because it is funny. I am laughing because it is not. I think I developed this irritating stress reaction from having to stay calm as a child and kneel next to my sister and count Mississippi's during her seizures. Driving a friend doubled over with kidney stones to the hospital once, I grinned and giggled terribly all the way to the emergency room. People get angry.

"You are the worst person to be around when something happens," Jake moaned. "Owwww . . ."

"I'm sorry," I said. "Look the other way."

"What are you going to do?"

"I think we have to pull it out."

The shed board was as long as a baseball bat. I grabbed either side. "Don't look," I said.

"Just do it."

"Stop looking at me like that," I said. "Don't make me laugh." I heaved. It came part way out, but it was still in his shoe.

"Okay. How's that?"

"Still in my foot!"

I pulled again and heard a small, bad sound. It was out. A long, rusty-shed nail. "Oh my God. Don't look," I said. "I got it."

"Let me see," he said, turning around. "Jesus."

I offered him a hand. Luckily we had gotten those tetanus and hepatitis shots.

"Come on," I said. "We should go. There's no water. We need to flush that out before it closes up. You don't want rust getting stuck in there."

Jake grabbed my arm.

"I'm going to vomit," Jake said.

"No, you're not."

"Yes, I am. Hold on a sec. I'm serious."

"Sit down a minute. But don't let it touch anything floody. It's filth over here."

"No, let's just go," Jake said. He shook his head once hard. "I'm done."

"Do you want to lean on me?" I said.

"I'm going to hop," he said.

"Don't hop on another nail. We both need to get some real boots."

One of the returning neighbors, an older man, cringed when he saw Jake hop into the front yard with his bloody sock foot behind him. Our block had gone from twenty houses broken into smaller apartments filled with much coming and going to a desolate rural road. The few of us there on any given day were now suddenly attuned to one another's presence.

"Nail," I called to the man so he wouldn't worry it was worse.

He nodded. Jake leaned up against the car. He inspected the bottom of his crimson sock.

"Hey chief," the neighbor called. "You're going to have to dig that out."

Jake blanched.

"Thanks," he waved.

As we drove back Uptown, Jake got worried. "I think it went in my bone. I wonder if I'm going to need a doctor," he said. "Call your mom and ask."

One benefit of having a nurse for a mother is that you can call and bug her day or night.

"When we get there," I said. "Hopefully we can just clean it. If it stops bleeding it's not an *emergency* emergency. Then there's the whole finding an open doctor thing."

Awhile back I had needed an antibiotic. Someone had told us with so many doctors and hospitals flooded and closed, a free Navy clinic ship, the USNS *Comfort,* had sailed to New Orleans and was open to the public. We went to the riverfront. We searched and searched and finally found it docked all the way back at the Poland Street Wharf where no one would think to look for it. But as we pulled up, the USNS *Comfort* pulled away, its shipmates grinning and waving bon voyage. Jake waved. They thought we had come to see them off.

The next day Jake could not walk. He hopped across the sublet with Clo barking and dive-bombing his raised foot for a week. Once Jake finished staring glassily through an entire box set of *Frasier* DVDs, he bought some steel-toed boots and was back on two feet. But he started acting funny. The nail had not infected his foot or given him a fever, but it was as if a tiny disaster germ had entered his bloodstream.

Jake blew off some video production work he had left, opting to mask up and help Tim wrestle soggy pink insulation from

Helen and Paul's house instead. We could not find an honest electrician to save our life, so Jake Googled an online electrician class.
I didn't want to sleep in a house wired by Jake, Your Internet Electrician. But both Dave and Tim thought this was a great idea.

Musicians Jake had been working with started to call, reestab-
lished somewhere else. They wanted to know if he intended to
finish their recording project. Jake told them instead about the
flooded but perfectly good box of glass tubes for amps he had
found on Bienville Street. If they were still listening, he would
launch into the unflooded stand-up bass someone put on the curb
Uptown as well as the rusted, red-and-blue seventies Vespa we
had rolled home from around the corner.

"Get this," Jake said. "It was underwater for three weeks and
the engine actually turned over."

Along with our neighbors, the flood washed away a lot of my
friends and acquaintances. Left was an odd mix of hardcores and
homegrowns. I was surprised at the way the flood brought friends
from high school back into my life on a regular basis.

The plan was to quarantine the high IQ and inexplicably artsy
from the general Louisiana populace into a two-year boarding
high school in north Louisiana's old plantation country. There we
teenagers could fester and feed one another's blossoming weird-
nesses in hopes of somehow saving our state. Portly Louisiana
politicians would visit and deliver grand and guilt-provoking
speeches. Like a judge or senator enjoying a comp trip to a Canal
Street brothel, when we kids had finished supping on Ovid at the
public trough, we had certain obligations. We owed them not to
flee the state.

Yes, we could take classes in Latin American politics and swap
mix tapes. We could strap on garbage bags and prance in one another's musicals. We could proclaim ourselves bisexuals or deliver
dorm-room lectures on SATs and foreskin. We could watch *Blade*

Runner in the lobby and *Monty Python* in the auditorium and quiz down Indian American friends about whether they would submit to arranged marriages. We could talk robot all night. Fine, fine, fine. But when we got through with all this, please remember to save the state. I had been a teen Louisiana ambassador there.

Michael was not a Louisiana ambassador, but he should have been. He was a chess wiz who could checkmate most of us in about five moves. Before my stuff flooded, I had a photo of Michael from high school, spinning in the air with his trench coat flying in the breeze. He was interested in flying rods, Alex the famous talking gray African parrot, and whether the Mayan calendar was right about the world ending in 2010.

Michael was lanky as ever with the same dark, shaggy hair. Being around Michael felt like continuity. One day we tossed most of his parents' belongings to the curb in New Orleans East, and another day he came over to Mid-City to help gut and critique my technique.

"Show me what you've been doing," he said.

I crashed my hammer sideways into the wall.

"Nope," Michael said. "Give me that. Wait. Don't give me that. Give me something bigger. A crowbar. This house is what? Three thousand square feet?"

"Almost," I said. "Thirteen rooms, four hallways. Some closets."

"Exactly. Twelve-foot ceilings and solid horsehair plaster? What you want to do is bring this down in the least number of strikes possible."

"A lot of it just crumbled," I said, pointing to the exposed studs where we had already gutted the walls to five or six feet.

"That sat in water for weeks. This is like solid brick," he said. "Rely on brute force to take a whole house like this out? You'll want to kill yourself first. What you want to do is convince the wall to take itself down."

"Ah, interesting," I said. "Respect the wall. Wall, will you please

take yourself down? Thank you for the hundred years. Your services are no longer required."

"You mock, but kind of, yeah," he said. "Ladder."

"Okay, but be careful. It flooded. You might break through."

"That's fine," he said. "And the crowbar. I'm about to save you
weeks of grief."

I took what Michael said about labor-saving seriously. He did
not believe in the forty or even thirty-hour workweek. For years
Michael worked less than I did, but somehow always seemed to
have his feet propped on the porch of a cheap apartment in a nicer
neighborhood. When I was in college, we drove all around New
Orleans collecting soil samples for a research project on lead.
Somehow I was the one who leaped into people's yards and shov-
eled a quick cup into a specimen bag while he sat in the car blasting old Hüsker Dü.

Michael climbed the ladder. "Start at the top and the force of
the wall coming down will pull more wall down with it," he said.
"Like this."

He popped the crowbar against the very top of the wall and a
big chunk of plaster loosened. He popped once more and half the
wall crashed to the floor in huge, scary chunks.

"Hey," I said, jumping back.

"See?" he grinned.

"Awesome. But you might just be hitting harder," I said. "Also
lucky swing."

"Of course I'm hitting harder. But I'm also hitting smarter. I
could be tapping it as light as you and still be doing less work," he
said, hopping off the ladder.

"Every time you touch this house you need to ask yourself
how you can work less. Think about the long haul."

He handed me the dusty crowbar.

"Every time you lift this, conserve your energy and harness
its."

"Ah. So let the force be with you," I said.

Michael smiled. "Exactly. Now time for a cigarette."

We walked out to the backyard.

"It looks like hell out here. Jeez. Look at that kitchen," he said, pointing to the two-story open dollhouse that loomed over our backyard. "There are still mugs in that cabinet."

He lit a cigarette and plopped down on Helen's newly disinfected glider. He took a long drag and swung slowly back and forth. "This glider is nice though," he said. "If you can get over the view. Salvage?"

"Kind of," I said. "Friend. On loaner maybe until they get back."

"Sweet," Michael said.

I sat down next to him. "Don't blow that on me," I said.

"You always say stuff like that," Michael said. "Why would I blow this on you? Don't worry. Relax. I have the perfect trajectory."

"Jake keeps saying he's going to take this electrician course on the Internet. He thinks he could learn it, become certified, and rewire the house quicker and cheaper than finding someone," I said.

"Sounds like a great idea."

"Does it?" I said.

Lately it was getting hard to tell what was a great idea and what was an idiotic one. Before the storm, saving an antique oak pedestal table from an unflooded curbside junk pile was a no-brainer, almost an obligation. But now dragging that same oak table into a messed-up filth-pit house before you even had walls seemed stupid.

"Is there any good reason Jake shouldn't be an electrician?" Michael said. "He does much more complicated things."

"How about I just don't like it?" I said.

"That's ridiculous. You would say that and call it a reason. At least you admit it." He took a long drag and expelled his smoke in an arc toward the dollhouse. "What's not to like?"

"Getting shocked. Wasting time. Getting more off track than we already are."

"I think it's brilliant. You shouldn't be so close-minded to perfectly simple solutions. After he's finished with your house, he could start rewiring other people's houses. He could make a killing just by being honest," Michael said. "How often does that happen? Maybe *I* should do it."

"Then you do it," I said.

"Nah,"Michael said. "Too much work. I need to show you these pew cushions I got. Red velvet. Unflooded. About thirty of them from a church in the Garden District. Just beautiful."

"Sounds great," I said. "But where are you going to put all that?"

Michael's apartment was high and dry on Magazine Street. Whenever I stopped by, a rotating crew of flooded people was crashed face-first on his sofa. I wasn't sure what all went on there. Once, when Michael was out of town and I knocked, some shirtless Turkish guys came to the door and yelled at me.

"I'm lining my bedroom," he said. "End to end. I'll leave a path."

"Picklewick and Lulu will be living the life," I said. Those were his pet rats. "They'll be swinging harem-style in their washcloth hammock above all that red velvet."

"Oh they'll be running all over it," Michael said. "I let them out."

you don't have to ask, do you?

I was working with a Canadian radio journalist who had come to town. Driving around through the expansive persistence of the mess, I found I did not have the stomach for sticking a microphone in a bunch of flooded faces to ask how they felt. I knew. They felt how I felt—only often a thousand times worse.

Jake and I were lucky. We were younger and healthier; we had each other, some insurance, and no kids. We had that mythical ruined upstairs and a short sublet. We were flailing some, but not going under.

Although crucial, money was not always the decisive factor. I had already seen a number of older, even elderly ladies gutting the hell out of ruined houses. I had seen large families begin to set things straight by marshalling pure cousin power. A lady on my street told me sheer rage was helping take down her walls. In post-flood New Orleans, whatever combination of gumption, family, anger, or naïveté enabled a person to pick up a hammer and at least hope was a new kind of gold.

The Canadian journalist wore big headphones and wielded a cartoon-size microphone. Even strapped into goofy headgear, he was Anderson Cooperesque, kind of nerdy debonair. He had flown in from Toronto and looked as if he was sleeping in a hotel with crisp linen sheets.

On Orleans Avenue, a heavyset woman in her sixties sat on a chair on her stoop mopping her forehead with the back of her hand. She was the only person we had seen for a mile. Piles of twisted clothes and furry sofas were beginning to litter the neutral ground.

Pulling over, I felt like a rat. I tried to remind myself that journalism served a purpose. Two teenagers peeked out of the little wood, shotgun-double house behind her. I waved and smiled. The boys waved back. Jake and I had noticed that everyone waved to each other in flooded neighborhoods now. Like when you got out of a car on a deserted rural road and were relieved to spot one single soul. The Canadian turned on his microphone. Mrs. S., the woman on the stoop, was disgusted.

"I just wish that we could get somebody to come help us to pull out all the stuff that's all soggy and mildew and been floating around," Mrs. S. said. "We have to pull out everything before we can even begin to try to, you know. To rebuild, you know . . . fix the house . . ."

"You don't have electricity?" the Canadian asked, glancing down to check his audio levels.

"We have *nothing*. Lamps and candles, lamps and candles. We in the dark and nothing. You know. Eating cold cuts and stuff."

I peeked in, hoping to see clean studs and rubble and camping stuff. Instead, I spotted mold scumming up the walls. Mrs. S. was sitting on her stoop so that she could breathe. The grandsons grinned nervously.

"You're *living* here now?" the Canadian asked. He knew what was going on, but still he seemed shocked.

"We have to. We don't have nowhere else to go. We' just trying to get help to drag stuff out. It's nobody around . . . nobody, nobody. You see the waterline. You see the floor all mildew. It's really not healthy to be in here but we have to come back. But we need help. I can't do anything . . . my little daughter can't do anything. She got two little teenagers. They not men. Need help. You know . . . just need *help*."

A few National Guardsmen suddenly appeared on the corner in their military truck. We all looked toward them.

"Come here," Mrs. S. commanded. "I'm trying to get help."

The soldier looked fresh out of high school, not much older than the skinny teens leaning against the house now acting cool. The soldier wrote down the grandmother's cell phone number. "I'll turn this in. And possibly somebody will come by and assess the damage and help you out," he said.

The National Guard, the grandsons, the Canadian, and I all stood there looking at one another dumbly. Mrs. S.'s adult daughter walked over from I didn't know where. Finally one of the children grabbed something and tossed it out.

The Canadian asked the soldier how that assistance might work and how long it would take.

The soldier shrugged. "I have no idea how long it's going to take," he said, strolling back to his corner.

Mrs. S. shook her head in disgust. She leaned over the stoop toward the Canadian. "You know the score. You know the score. This is the name of the game. Okay? Nobody cares for you when you're down and out and of color. Okay? You know this is a racist society. You read the papers . . . you see TV. You know. You know. You don't have to ask, do you?"

The Canadian wondered what New Orleans had tasted like, but not much was open or the same. We went to eat at Joey K's. After seeing all the families sleeping in their mold, the gumbo looked pretty thin.

real progress

I was the kind of person who whipped up vegetarian red beans and rice, vegetarian muffalettas, and perhaps most scandalous, a vegetarian gumbo with an organic pot likker and roux. My friends thought these were all great. Mom did not. She cooked traditional Hungarian and Louisiana food, neither particularly revered for their life-extending qualities.

But after many heart-saving years of vegetarianism in New Orleans, I had reverted to catfishatarianism and brought Jake crashing down with me. I had no good reason for this change. I had noticed an epidemic of fleur-de-lis and NOLA FOREVER tattoos beginning to sweep unflooded New Orleans, claiming many suddenly emblazoned victims. After the storm, maybe eating a catfish po boy felt like waving your Bienvenue en Lousiane flag. Or coming running home after having your butt kicked.

Mom was happy I was backsliding. I'd moved away at fifteen and grown more unintentionally inexplicable every year since. Sometimes when I was talking she looked at me and shook her head. But po-boys were like Esperanto. On her second mission into the quagmire, Mom cruised by Middendorf's at Manchac on her way over. She came bearing po-boys and the dogs jumped up to greet her.

"Sorry. Nothing for you two today," Mom said. "This is a nice place. How long do you have it?"

"A little bit," I said.

"How long?" Mom said, sounding worried.

I shrugged. "We'll figure something out. Let's eat on the porch away from these beggars."

Jake came out to join us and shut the door against the dogs. Clo barked.

"Hello, hello," Mom said to Jake. "How's your foot?"

"I'm walking," Jake answered.

"Hurray! Now buy some boots."

"I did," Jake said.

A few bites into our sandwiches, the pesky flies descended.

Mom rewrapped her po-boy in butcher paper and started slapping the air. "Shoo!" she said. "Shoo!"

There was nothing worse than post-flood flies. They were a plague on our porch on the Isle of Denial.

"Some entomologists called these coffin flies," I told Jake. "Remind me to tell Jack."

"Yuck," Mom said, shooing even harder. She stood up. "Give me a magazine."

I went inside and returned with a rolled-up newspaper. "We can go inside," I said. "It's been going on for a while. Not a battle you're going to win."

"Oh, never mind. I'll just cover it up between bites." Mom sighed, sneaking a bite around the edge of the paper.

Soon the sky darkened and it began to drizzle.

"Do you think we should go check on the house?" I asked Jake.

"Too late now," Jake said. "We should have done it this morning."

"We should have done it yesterday before we left."

"Well, I didn't know it was going to rain," Jake said.

"There's a forty percent chance," Mom informed us.

Jake looked like he bit into a bad shrimp.

"What?" Mom said.

"FEMA untarped our roof," I said.

"What do you mean untarped your roof? That doesn't make any sense."

"Exactly," I acknowledged, taking another bite of the po-boy.

I didn't feel like talking about it. I felt like fixing it or not. It was too aggravating to talk about.

"The people who are supposed to help keep breaking stuff we'll have to fix," Jake said. "The bobcats knocked down the rest of our front fence. They broke the neighbor's water meter. Now FEMA untarped the roof."

Some days the street would rumble and suddenly our desolate corner of the 70119 dump would spring to life. When the white-suited Hazmat guys and gals blocked off the corner and their traffic flags dropped, all bets were off. You better jump on the porch. Orange-vesters in mirrored sunglasses revved their bobcat engines, and the tiny, miserable demolition derby would begin. Forward and backward like bumper cars they went, sorting the garbage piles.

Some of the drivers were careful, but others were crazy. Jake was afraid they would crash our only remaining car. He would rush in shouting, "They're back! Where are your keys?"

Sometimes I stood on the porch in my gas mask and kept an eye on the workers. Pastor Jim, a freelance minister with a tattoo of a lecherous wolf panting on his bicep, owned two properties on our street. He saw me watching one day. "Good," he said. "Keep watching. Don't let them break my other meter."

One day Jake and I journeyed to the workmen's mothership. Across from where people used to picnic in City Park, a kind of Garbage City had emerged, complete with trailers, kitchens, and tents. As we parked in a tangle of dump trucks near Phillips and Jordan's command central, a woman who appeared to be an elderly prostitute emerged from one of the contractor pup tents, smoking a cigarette and adjusting her short-shorts. I wondered whether this type of hospitality team always traveled with them.

Jake and I asked why garbage guys were breaking things and not showing up for weeks, and when someone was going to pick up all the dead dogs. But we left with no good answers. Mysteries remained. Why did some burly disaster contractors strap gigantic teddy bears to the front of their dump trucks? And who were the men we saw that night?

One evening at about ten o'clock Jake and I had to brave the darkness and go back to our house for something we had forgotten. As we turned the corner, a dump truck roared up out of the pitch black and two men jumped out. Under the thick cover of night and their own gritty plaster dust cloud, they grabbed some water heaters out of one of the "white goods" appliance piles, tossed it into the back of their dump truck, and sped off. Rumor had it these were pissed-off, renegade contractors passed over in the great debris contract giveaway. But no one really knew.

"I don't understand," Mom said. "Did you ask them to tarp your roof or not?"

"Months ago," Jake said. "But they never came. We did the twenty-foot roof but we needed them to do the second-story one. When they finally came and tarped the top roof, they untarped the bottom roof and never retarped it."

Mom shook her head. "Can't you just call them?"

Jake laughed a new, bitter laugh. "You can. And I do. But it doesn't help."

"Keep calling," Mom said.

"He *does*," I snapped, not meaning to. "All the time."

People outside the flood zone kept insisting that help was a mere phone call away. It was not. They found it hard to believe, so they kept insisting, saying, "Can't you just call?" or "Hey, I have an idea. Why don't you just call?" over and over. People's refusal to believe it was exhausting. Like rats in some God-awful experiment, we pressed the lever repeatedly. But we got a shock more often than a pellet.

"They use different contractors," Jake said. "So no one ever knows exactly what is going on. They have some for regular, some for slate."

"You can't nail a tarp on slate," I said. "First they were sending out contractors to bust people's slate."

"Lucky you don't have slate," Mom said.

She then put down her po-boy in disgust. "I can't eat with these flies," she said. "If we're going to go, let's go."

"I'm not getting on the roof today," Jake said.

I stood up and brushed off the crumbs. "We can at least shut the windows," I said.

We were trying to dry out the studs like I'd learned at the disaster mold seminars. But a neighbor claimed we were just letting other people's mold spores blow in.

"I want to show you what we got done," I told Mom.

Mom nodded but looked a little queasy. "Okay," she said. "But only for a second."

"Oh. I didn't know you had to drive back early."

"No," she said. "I just hadn't planned on going over *there*."

Driving under the I-10 at Carrollton, I was relieved someone had removed the abandoned boats and some of the mattresses. But Mom did not notice the improvement. As we crossed Tulane Avenue, she frowned.

"They didn't get those cars yet?" she said. "I thought they would have at least gotten those cars!"

"They moved that mound of rotten clothes out of the parking lot of Thrift City," I offered, embarrassed. "A band just played Rock 'n' Bowl."

It was crazy, but true. You couldn't even see Mid-City from the interstate anymore. All the lights were out so it was pitch black like driving over Lake Pontchartrain. As if our neighborhood had been wiped off the face of the map. I didn't go hear the music, but I was glad someone sent a song up over the sadness. I heard it was Eddie Bo.

I hoped Mom turned and did not drive all the way up to Canal Street. If she did, we would have to turn by the kidney dialysis machines still on the curb. And she would discover that the Robért grocery building could barely be seen at all. It was obscured behind a fantastical, block-long heap of flooded and now putrefied groceries.

I gritted my teeth and glanced at Jake. He must have read my mind.

"Turn here," he said.

Mom turned right just in time. But piloting her sedan through a narrow gap in the piles of crap clotting Palmyra Street, she spotted a flooded pickup truck filled like an overflowing Dumpster near a toppled tree. She gasped. She stopped the car.

"It looks worse!" she cried. "Is that possible?"

"They're not really picking it up lately," Jake admitted. "They're just kind of spreading it around."

I realized I should give it up. Obviously our very real and very difficult progress at cleaning and gutting our house would not look at all like real progress to my mother. My only hope now was to get out of the afternoon without any sobbing. What had I been thinking?

Mom looked anxious as she searched for a path between Jake's flooded van, a heap of mossy linoleum, and several rotting meat freezers to pick her way into our house.

"I don't see how y'all don't break your necks," she said. "I better not get a nail!"

After a five-minute progress tour of our gutted and mostly disinfected house, I brought Mom upstairs and showed her a temporary repair I was kind of proud of.

"Look, I hauled the wall off the floor from where the wind

blew it in and tacked Visqueen over the hole," I said. "We'll prob-ably have to take the whole wall out. But now it's not raining in."

Mom was not impressed. She put her hand in the air like one of those flags the orange-vesters use to redirect traffic. I had the distinct sense she wanted us to dump the house.

"I've seen enough!" she said, and turned around and marched down the stairs.

We and the few neighbors who had begun to work early had really and truly inched forward. That's why the streets looked like tunnels cut through blocks of garbage. Jake and I had already removed an actual ton of belongings, sludge, walls, and debris. We had made progress. Apparently just none that the unflooded eye could see. I was going to show Dave my wall patch.

Chapter 13

ka-chunk

"Why can't he stay in Austin?" I said. "I thought we were good for at least a little longer."

"It's his apartment," Jake said.

The poet's life reminded me of my old life—only with a dishwasher, a private study instead of a band practice room, and central air. I was bummed that he wanted it back. I moaned and wailed and cursed the poet, rolling around on his boyfriend's bed.

"I thought they liked it there. Why won't they just stay another month? God, he sucks," I said. "It's cold."

"He's probably sick of being away for so many months," Jake said. "You'd be, too."

There were few unflooded apartments. We could not find a place that allowed the dogs. I would not be able to live with myself if I sent Clo to my mother's backyard for the winter. Clo had stayed there one weekend when she was young, and Lori had left the front door open. Clo had run smack into a car, rolled, then kept running. A few days later, Mom opened the front door to find Clo had returned, sitting quietly on the front steps. But now Clo was elderly. Her eyes were hazy and she had frequent UTIs. She would never survive.

We could not tell how long our freelance employment would remain feasible in a smaller New Orleans, so it seemed foolish to sign a year's lease. I didn't want to get evicted for dog hiding and owe someone a year's rent. Above all, I refused to hand over fistfuls of money to one of the greedmongers who had jacked the rent to stick it to flooded people. Those apartments should sit empty. I hoped they would rot.

I stopped wallowing and sat up in bed. If taking the hit was inevitable, and it was looking like it might be, I needed to adjust my attitude. Quick.

"Of course maybe if we're staying there it'll be so terrible that we'll work quicker. We won't have anywhere to run to," I said. "Maybe we can slam it out. Work at night, too."

"Work on what? We can't work all night without lights. What can we slam out if we can't get an electrician to come?"

"Use our new generator," I said.

"Doesn't matter. There's an order. You can't close any walls until the wire's in them. Can't hang Sheetrock until after inspection. Can't do floors until after Sheetrock."

"We could get a head start on *something*," I said. "I can list ten things right now that still need to be done, electrician or not."

Jake dropped down on the bed next to me. I flopped back down beside him. We both stared at the ceiling.

"You say that now," he said. "But the only reason you can deal with this at all is because you get to come Uptown every night."

"I can deal with it fine," I said. "The only reason *you* can deal with it is because *you* get to come Uptown at night."

"I know," Jake said. "That's my point."

In theory, we could get a FEMA trailer. In reality, FEMA had already accidentally bumped Jake from the list. We had discovered this when we called to check on the status. Jake and I were supposedly back on the list, but the way FEMA had been untarping and losing people from lists, I felt like if they ever brought the trailer, something weird might happen.

"Can we get ourselves off the trailer list?" I said.

"Probably when I call to check next week we'll find out the computer already bumped us again."

"Maybe that's a good thing. Let's officially get off the list."

"You're serious?"

"Yeah."

"No. That's silly. Do you have any idea how many broken windows we have to replace? Not to mention the siding and holes in the walls. Upstairs is shit. We're going to have to take down your Visqueen and gut the rest for the electricians. How cold do you think it's going to be then?"

"I'm scared of the trailer," I said.

"That's ridiculous."

"Not to be all Ruby Ridge, but I just really think we should minimize our contact with the government wherever possible. Every time they mess stuff up it makes extra work for us."

"Yeah. But what else could they do?"

"They could literally drive us crazy."

"Nah," Jake said.

"They could decide in three months to charge us for the trailer somehow even though now they're saying they won't. They could not hook something up right and gas us or something."

It wasn't beyond the pale. The trailer business was chaos. There were people with trailers but without keys and people with keys but without trailers. There were sewer pipes attached to nothing and temp poles attached to nothing and trailers without sewer pipes or temp poles. One day you were on the list; one day you were off. I did not trust them.

"I don't know if they could do that," Jake said. "Charge you afterward. Seems you could fight that kind of thing."

"But then you'd be stuck fighting it. Another thing they could do and probably *will* do is finally bring the trailer but then refuse

to take it away. Think about it. Are they truly going to get orga-
nized in the next six months? By then it'll just be sitting there in
the way of some scaffolding we need or something."

"Oh they're going to do that," Jake said. "Definitely."

"Then what if it floods next summer? They won't have fixed
the Seventeenth Street Canal or anything by then. It'll flood,
but only flood enough to float the trailer and knock it into the
house."

"Now you're over-thinking it. If it floods next summer, we're
free. I will dump this shit so fast it'll make your head spin."

"Really?" I said.

"Yeah."

I knew how he felt, but the words still sounded funny coming
out of Jake's mouth. That summer Jake had still loved his big,
old New Orleans house, even if it did need fixing. Its space had
given him the freedom to have a music room and sometimes let
friends move in. But in a few short months the house had become
a two-story ball and chain.

"I don't want to get shot on the sidewalk sleeping in the garbage in some trailer," I said. "There's no room for the dogs."

"Who's going to shoot you in your trailer?"

"I don't know. It feels like sleeping in a car. Would you sleep in
your car on our street before the flood?"

"No," Jake said. "But there's nobody around now."

"Except You-Know-Who."

"Oh yeah," Jake said. "Fuck."

You-Know-Who was the Armed Rapist. When the notice first
came out in the paper years earlier, I called him Armed Rapist.
Like, "Oh, I saw your good buddy Armed Rapist biking by today.
He said to tell you hey." But since we had spotted him back living
upstairs in an ungutted house with no electricity a block away,
one of the few people actually sleeping in Mid-City for blocks, I

had reduced the charges to You-Know-Who. The sex crimes parolee had just as much right to return to his flooded upstairs as we did. But I no longer felt like being progressive and magnanimous and all benefit-of-the-doubt about it. It just sucked.

I turned sideways in the bed and watched the tree branches moving outside the window. They had lost their leaves.

"We're lucky they let us stay here," I said. "That really saved us. We'd be like those poor people driving in and out of town every day."

The disaster commuters were a sad sight to behold. Twice a day, they were braving hours of slow, dangerous, emotionally distraught, and sleep-deprived drivers and FEMA trailers on wheels to go to work and then wrangle workers or fix their own houses. Looking ahead a year, it seemed impossible to believe that they would have enough money or energy left to see the thing through. Maintaining a foothold in the city seemed essential to ultimate success. Shutters, doors, copper plumbing, iron gates, architectural details—you name it—thieves were stripping anything people had left from houses every day.

I attempted to be rational. We would be cold. Meals and hygiene would be a hassle. But what was I really afraid of? It was like bedlam, but it was not like living in bedlam was contagious.

One day, we saw an old man riding a bicycle pulling a laughing old woman on a hospital gurney behind him. There weren't many other people around. The old gurney couple did not seem like a good sign.

And the forgotten family we had found right after the storm had returned. Just in time for winter, some lack-of-social-service system had dumped the family back into the flood zone with their mental illness, no electricity, and no potable water. One cold black night, Jake and I had to return to our house to pick up something we had forgotten. In our headlights we saw them a block away—

two wild-haired women hosing down the developmentally disabled, naked teen in the street.

But these were not the only people. Dave and Marcelle had left
their upstairs for a sublet Uptown. But a twenty-something granola gal and her older boyfriend were staying in a travel camper
on a corner a few blocks away. Several men within a block claimed
FEMA was one day soon going to bring them a trailer. We would
be settlers like them. Not gurney people.

We were in Academy Sports off of Jefferson Highway. Past the
jock straps and the headbands and protein powders and yoga
pants into the nether regions of the sporting goods section. By
the gun case.

Ka-chunk!

"Everyone knows this sound," the clerk said, racking the shotgun from behind the glass counter. "Make this sound, chances
are you won't have to use this. Of course, if you're looking for
something more sporting . . ."

"We have to move back into the upstairs of our flooded house,"
I said. "We don't need anything sporty."

"Seriously?" the guy said.

"Yep," Jake answered.

He shook his head and whistled. "I'm sorry to hear it."

"Did you get any water?" I said.

"Nah. I live out this way," the clerk said, meaning Jefferson
Parish. "I wouldn't want to be in your shoes."

Jake shrugged.

"We want something that we'll hopefully never have to use or
accidentally kill ourselves with," I said. "Do you have anything
like that?"

He nodded, becoming excited. Like now there was a bona fide
mission to this sale. Probably he knew someone flooded. Every-

one did. Maybe selling us the perfect firearm was his way of setting all the upside-down right. If so, that was pretty messed up, yet I appreciated the gesture.

"All right," he said. "This is what we're going to do. Are you going to apply for a concealed permit so you can carry?"

Jake shook his head. "I don't think so. Nothing like that."

"It's more so we can sleep at night," I said, wondering if having a gun in the house itself would keep me awake.

"Then forget those," he said, waving off his glass counter filled with handguns.

The clerk turned and pulled another rifle from the wall behind him. This one was long, powder black, and thick. "Remington Magnum," he said. "Do you have a staircase?"

"Yeah," Jake said.

The salesman pointed the gun at the ceiling of Academy Sports. *Ka-chunk!* The sound gave me a cold metal shiver. He pumped it again and smiled. *Ka-chunk!* "You just stand at the top of the stairs and make this little music," he said. "I guarantee it's the world's most recognizable song."

I was hoping we'd never have to sing that tune. I was starting to think that moving back to Mid-City was a bad idea.

"Our staircase is kind of narrow though with a turn," I said. "You can't really see down it."

"Especially with no lights," Jake said.

"All the better," the guy said. "No offense, but you two don't strike me as the types who want to get in a shooting match."

He handed the shotgun to Jake. Jake sighted it and racked the pump. *Ka-chunk!* I had never seen Jake do that before. Jake grinned at the guy behind the counter. I had a weird feeling that Jake might be enjoying himself.

I didn't know if I believed in ka-chunk. One time a friend of mine had woken up with a guy going through her dresser. She pretended she was asleep until he left. Another time when I lived

on Lowerline, my roommate heard the cat bell and woke up to
a guy with a knife trying to pry open our upstairs porch door.
He grinned at my roommate and climbed back out the hole he
had slit in the porch screen. Both stories ended peacefully without
ka-chunk.

But now Jake was smiling and flipping his gun. When he
gripped the handle, I saw he had written a reminder on the back
of his fist. Where in the past he usually had an almost permanent
door stamp from seeing bands, he'd written GUN in big block let-
ters.

"Does that backfire?" I said.

"Not usually," the clerk said, winking. "Let me show you one
other that might do the trick."

"I'll be back," I said.

We needed lanterns, coldproof sleeping bags, a propane stove,
propane, and God knows what else. I wandered past As Seen on
TV! fat burners and ab loungers until I found the plastic kayaks
and dog life preservers. It had not been raining much, but the
levees and canal walls still weren't fixed. The pumps were down
and the catch basins throughout the city were clogged with storm
debris. Probably would be for months.

Jake and I could swim. But with so many neighbors returning
to tell me who had or had not floated on what, I had been wondering what would happen to the dogs should another flood come.
Clo and Buster had squat basset legs and could swim only pitifully
before tiring. Dog life preservers—I wondered—reasonable part
of emergency kit or tinfoil hat thought? Hard to tell. I was evacuated for this big flood, but twice before in New Orleans I'd found
myself wading in thigh-deep water. Once my friend's Toyota had
flooded to the hood and we had floated a few feet.

When Jake lugged the cardboard gun box and ammo out
past the protein bars and jogging bras to the checkout, I felt
stupid. As we drove away, I turned to Jake. "Have you ever

even used a gun?" I asked. I wondered why I hadn't thought of this before.

Jake swung the car out of the parking lot.

"Sure, a twenty-two a bunch of times," Jake said. "Do you want to go get that other stuff now? Like batteries?"

"I guess. When did you shoot a twenty-two?"

"When I was a kid."

"For what?"

"Nothing really. I just went out with Pop in Georgia," Jake said.

Pop was Jake's grandfather. He was on the first Florida State football team. Though Jake had never lived in Georgia, whenever he got on the phone with Pop he developed a mild Georgia accent like it was contagious. When Jake was a kid Pop drove a truck with a bumper sticker that said THIS TRUCK PROTECTED BY A PIT BULL WITH AIDS. At some point in the recent past, Pop had supposedly told Jake's mom that he liked me, which surprised me.

Once when visiting a friend's grandfather in McComb, Mississippi, I had helped myself to some green beans but passed on the fried chicken and had to confess to being vegetarian. My friend's grandfather had narrowed his eyes and smiled. "Ah-huh," he had said. "I knew there was something wrong with you, but I just didn't know what."

In a way, I took him to be speaking for all rural Southern men of a certain generation, including Pop. Over a lifetime of trying to communicate with friends' relatives with my somewhat unplaceable accent, I had grown accustomed to suspicion. I always had to "yes, ma'am" it harder than anyone else. And it didn't always work. But Pop liked me. Apparently I had been grandfathered in as a character. That's the slot reserved in Southern families for liberal or gay or non-football-watching relatives.

"Ah, Pop and little Jake and his twenty-two," I said. "What did you shoot?"

"We didn't shoot anything. I think the goal was probably to shoot some birds, but we never did," Jake replied. "I also shot a shotgun once at camp to shoot skeet. I never hit any."

My father had hunted, but I never accompanied him. When he died, left-behind deer antlers were still hanging on our wall and a few empty rifles lay stowed in the back of a closet. Mom didn't like these firearms but couldn't throw them away.

"No one took me hunting because I was a girl," I said. "But you know Mom never met a safety class she didn't like. So I did take a BB gun safety."

"We'll need to go to a firing range," Jake said. "Maybe I'll call Dave."

"Yeah, call Dave. I'm not going to any firing range," I said. "Can you even take a shotgun to a firing range?"

"I don't know. But it's stupid to have something you don't even know how to fire," Jake said.

"I don't want this turning into some kind of lifestyle," I said.

"Too late," Jake said.

"What's that supposed to mean?"

"It means it's a little late for that. I thought we already decided."

"You did," I said.

"*You* did," he countered.

"Whatever. I wouldn't be doing this alone."

"There's a lot I wouldn't be doing if it was just me," Jake affirmed. "Believe me."

"Don't go around telling everyone we got a gun," I said. "Maybe Dave, but that's it."

"Who would I tell?"

"Anybody. If you don't mind. Just don't. I don't want to hear a bunch of speeches. Half of the people we know won't even drive anywhere that flooded because it's too scary or depressing. Have you noticed that practically no one back has come to see us? And that's just the half that would give the speech."

"I could give a shit at this point," Jake said.

"That's not true."

"It really is," Jake said.

"Well, that's new," I said. "And not in a good way."

"So," Jake said.

"Well, I have to live in this town. I don't want anyone who just sat outside Rue guzzling iced coffee all day Googling up some gun-dot-org to show me," I said. "And don't tell Mom, either."

"Why would I?"

"Just don't," I said. "She's in our business since the flood. And I don't want to hear about it."

One reason Mom didn't like guns was because of the gun-related deaths in her family. Her cousin had died as a child when he and an NOPD policeman's son had been playing with the dad's pistol. And her grandmother stepped outside once to stop two men from arguing by grabbing their shotgun and banging it on the ground. The gun fired and killed her. After my grandfather died, we found a very old photograph with a man's face scratched out. "That's one of the men in that argument," Mom had said.

If Mom knew we had gotten a gun, she would think I was turning mose. Worse, a *vad* mose. *Mose* was a Hungarian Settlement slur that no one knew how to spell. A Cajun wasn't a mose. An Italian wasn't a mose. Someone French or German wasn't a mose. A New Orleanian wasn't a mose. A mose was a wild, uncivilized, barbarous American—sometimes poor, sometimes not. And maybe I was a mose now with our shotgun and flooded house of filth. But it wasn't all my fault.

"I won't tell your mom about the gun and you don't tell my mom about the chicken," Jake said.

"Deal," I said.

In desperation recently, Jake had fallen farther down the catfishatarian slippery slope. He had eaten some nasty disaster chicken dinner off a relief truck. He and his mother had become vegetarians together when he was ten. Brenda came from small-town Georgia, but over time the hippies in Gainesville had rubbed off some. In the eighties Gainesville was probably the only place in north Florida where you could buy nutritional yeast.

Between the shotgun and the chicken, I guess we were armed and ready. Hopefully for nothing.

Chapter 14

citizen loser

David and Courtney were a rare breed among artists: they still liked and vacationed with their parents. A few years back, in their old New Orleans corner store turned art studio, David taught tai chi to his mother and some of her friends. But now David's parents had flooded in Lakeview and moved out of state. Courtney's mom's house got smashed in Mississippi. But Courtney and David were high and dry in the Irish Channel in New Orleans trying to get back to their art.

David made tongue-in-cheek video games about capitalism and his own virtual immortality. Courtney created video projections of burning ballerinas, unraveling mummies, and women making spectacles of themselves. They would humor me when I called at odd hours with vague art notions. Before the flood, Courtney and Helen made a short film starring New Orleans termites.

But now Courtney wanted to drop by with her camera. I didn't want to see myself on a gallery wall as some candlelit metaphor for an ineffectual government and its equally ineffectual citizen loser. I wanted to see myself as somebody who took care of her little family and got her house fixed quickly.

"There's not much to document," I said into the cell phone.

"What . . ." she crackled.

The phone towers were not working right. From our block of the flood zone you could only hear about every other word.

Sometimes not even that. If we wanted to phone the unflooded world and have them hear us, we drove to the other side of the interstate.

"You won't have enough light," I said. "It's mostly candles. The generator's too loud and we have to run it outside because of the fumes. We don't use it at night."

". . . flash . . . here . . . David's parents' house . . . drive . . ." she said.

"Start over," I said. "Repeat everything!"

"Spooky . . . minute . . . way . . ." she crackled.

"Wait," I said.

"See you!" she said.

Jake was flat on his back on a mattress on the floor wearing a dollar knit hat pulled down low. Both sleeping bags were spread on top of him, and two hound heads poked out from under the covers by his feet. A cheap lantern on a cardboard box cast a weak blue glow. He was sucking peppermints. The room smelled of propane and Altoids.

"Did you leave the stove on?"

"I don't think so," Jake said. "Check."

I walked over to the little typing table by the window. When we turned on the propane stove, we opened the window for ventilation. The stove looked to be off.

"I don't hear any hissing. Maybe it just stinks from earlier," I said. "I think David and Courtney are coming over."

Jake flattened his book on his chest. "You're kidding," he said. "Why?"

"I don't know. I think she might want to take a picture," I said. "I think she's working on some project."

"What?" Jake said. "I'm not standing up. It's cold as shit."

No one came to Mid-City at night if they didn't have to. The I-10 Carrollton overpass marked where civilization ended and the road dipped. Losing the sublet was like getting kicked out of wine-and-garden New Orleans to the outback. It was going okay. Except sometimes we would hear the forgotten family's aunt scream *"Abuser!"* We would step outside to see the bedraggled figures clutching flooded stuffed animals from gutting piles. The aunt would collapse in a heap or she and the teenager would trade slaps as they walked up our deserted street.

"I was going to say no but I want to be nice. We might need to go over there for a shower," I said.

"Can they even find us?" Jake wondered. "Are we supposed to wait outside with a lantern?"

I hadn't thought of that. We tried to minimize our time outside. No streetlights.

"They can count streets from the corner. They'll see my car in their headlights. We should probably wait downstairs," I said.

"Sucks," Jake said.

Downstairs was construction zone and mouse zone. Avoiding being downstairs and outside at night made things more tolerable. Yes, you were two people in a cold room with a tarped wall and two dogs, but there was the glow of candles and jokes. On good nights we felt perched and even snug above the fray. Out our bedroom window, you could see downtown glittering like Emerald City in the distance.

On bad nights, putting on your shoes and walking with a candle to the bathroom felt like venturing out into the bleak. If Jake forgot something in the car, he brought the shotgun along. If the dogs had to pee, he brought the shotgun. I hoped a neighbor didn't forget a tool, drive back to their empty house one night, and see Jake lurking with the shotgun.

Jake flipped his book back up off his chest. "They're your guests, not mine," he said.

"I'll tell her she can document Clo and Buster," I offered.

"Maybe she just wants to take a picture of the setup," Jake said. "And she's going to animate something around it."

I thought about that. Mold spores, big pink hearts, prancing Mardi Gras spears. Rising or falling water. Who knew? I didn't fully trust artists. Some writers I knew had stuck me on a page and made me dance around before, but they could only go so far. They didn't have animation software.

"What could she do with a photo of a propane stove and some Cup Noodles?" I said.

Jake shrugged.

Even though I was getting bored on our island, I wasn't in the mood to host some disaster salon. Jake and I had been taking turns reading *Pimp: The Story of My Life* by Iceberg Slim aloud for entertainment, but then I became depressed from all the slapping. We were planning to get a battery-operated satellite radio boom box. Then before bed we could gaze out our big back window at the downtown lights and get out of Mid-City for a while by listening to chipper voices from England instead.

"I'm sick of art people," I said. "Why don't we know a single plumber or electrician? My appreciation for the usefulness of aesthetics is at an all-time low."

That wasn't totally true. A guy named Jonathan had floated around the flood in an innertube taking photographs. After the water subsided, he had erected photographic signs all around Bayou St. John and Mid-City. I wasn't sure if it was supposed to be commentary or art or public information. But stumbling upon his flashback signs one day had been a small revelation. Near where we'd returned to find a crashed helicopter, he had erected a large photo of a working helicopter landing to pick up people stranded near a hospital. The people were crowded onto a slim strip of dry green grass in the middle of a lake that had since disappeared. His photos illustrated my returning neighbor's stories.

"Maybe they're just coming to check on us," Jake said. "You're just grumpy because the camping is messing up your sleep."

"Duh," I said.

"When our electricity is back, I'm going to hang Christmas lights outside so people can see, if these streetlights don't get fixed. Should I clean up?"

"It's as good as it's going to get," Jake said.

I had our bedroom-kitchen-kennel pretty disinfected, but the daily film of plaster dust always returned. I wound up baby-wiping dust off my arms and out of the dogs' long ears a lot. One toilet worked, and we had running water in the yard. We had paper plates and plastic forks, but washing the one pot we had was a problem. I didn't want flood-zone tap water touching anything that touched anything we ate. We brushed our teeth with bottled water. Other solutions included eating instant cheese grits and the dreaded Cup Noodles, taking vitamins, and driving Uptown to get a sandwich.

Someone suggested that we join the Jewish Community Center so that we could stop bumming showers from friends. You didn't have to be Jewish. A lot of the members weren't back yet and the center was running specials. I was going to look into it.

We had been talking a lot about how to budget stress so we would have reserves for the long run. A documentarian Jake had worked with had recently shot himself in his flooded house about six blocks away. Some people said it was because the storm had destroyed his life's work, others said it was because FEMA brought the wrong trailer; and others said it was because he was camping out in his upstairs. We didn't know.

I doubt many of us had ever been under this many different types of stress for so long. Some days Jake and I were both in rotten moods. Other days we took turns.

Whenever another flooded someone killed himself, I hoped that the mind was not like a camel's back waiting for its last straw. I did not feel that bad, considering. But maybe none of the other people had felt that bad, either. Maybe people just woke up one day and some bureaucrat or nail in the foot sent them over the edge. Basic rebuilding information was in constant flux. The stream of misinformation, correction, and re-misinformation was brutal, so anything seemed possible.

Learning how to free your ankle all day, every day, from a seemingly never-ending series of booby traps was crucial. We inaugurated the Get Aggravated the Fifth Time, Not the Third method. But then we quickly had to up that five to ten. It wasn't exactly like letting go, though it was. It felt more like learning to take a hit.

So when the hammer breaks in your hand and you drive to the hardware store to replace it but the hardware store flooded and never reopened and you finally find a place that is open and you have to get a thirty-dollar hammer or no hammer at all and you suck that up and grab the last one and head to the checkout and the telephone is still out so they only take cash and you go to the ATM and it's smashed and then you finally somehow, someway get cash and go back and get that golden hammer but also a nail in your tire, don't get mad. Just take the deepest breath of your life and figure out how to get that tire fixed. When you go back home to discover you're thirsty and out of bottled water and that Clo ate some plaster, shit it on your mattress, and Buster ate it, *then* go throw some bricks at the collapsing shed. *Then* cry like a baby into Clo's fur.

So what that five hours have passed and you only managed to replace a hammer? Call it a day. Go find a friend's shower hopefully and briefly collapse on her warm sofa afterward instead. Lather, rinse, repeat.

So far this plan was kind of working. And some days when it did fail, a neighbor or a complete stranger would stop his car, get out, and help you pull your ankle from some trap. Thank you, New Orleans.

"I think I hear a car," I said.

Jake threw off the covers. He still had on his coat and his shoes under there. The dogs stretched.

"Okay," he said. "I'll go down ahead. Grab both lanterns."

In the dim light, I could see David and Courtney on the front porch, bundled up. Courtney's curly hair spilled from her winter hat.

"You're our first nighttime visitors," Jake said.

"Is that good or bad?" David asked.

"You tell us," I said. "Come on, let's go up. It's mousy down here."

Courtney's eyes widened.

Jake held his lantern high at the front and I held mine high at the back of our little line.

"Be careful," Jake said. "Watch that glass. Walk here."

We picked around the sawhorses and ladders and mess.

"Don't let those nails grab you," I said. "Stay away from the wall."

At the back of the house, near the bottom of the stairwell, Jake stopped and said, "We got the floor leveled. Can you tell?"

Courtney laughed. "Looks great!"

"Oh wait, you're serious," David said. He turned around and squinted back into the dark front rooms. "You mean you raised the house?"

"A few inches," Jake said. "We're already at supposed elevation. We just had it leveled."

"The flood made it sink more in the middle," I explained. "You have to do things in a certain order. If you level it after you put on the roof, then it makes the roof leak. We didn't realize we were going to have to level it."

"Well in that case it looks very nice and flat," David said. "Really, I can't see anything."

"Tim found somewhere where the crew forgot to tie it back

into the foundation," Jake said. "The house was just floating. We had to get them to come back."

"Good old Tim," Courtney said.

"No kidding," Jake said. "I never would have noticed that."

We walked up the narrow staircase, our shadows twisting alongside.

"It would be nice not to pay money to make it worse," David said.

"Tell me about it," Jake said.

I opened the bedroom door. "This is where the magic happens. Tea?" I said. "Actually we have a French press if you want coffee. Zapp's? Vitamins? Cup Noodles? I'm afraid that's it."

"I'm okay," Courtney said.

"Well, it's cozy," David added.

"That's one word for it," Jake said.

I motioned toward the plastic chair. "Here, David, seat of honor. You probably want your coat."

"Why, thank you," he said, settling in. "I can see my breath nicely."

"It's warm once you're in bed," I said.

Courtney pulled her camera from her bag.

"That's what I thought you said on the phone, but I couldn't hear. You can take some pictures of the dogs if you feel like it," I offered. "And Jake. Not me."

"Not me, either," Jake said. "I'll pass."

"It's not our finest hour," I pointed out. "I don't want to look stupid."

"You won't look stupid," Courtney said.

"Still," I countered, "human photography ban."

Courtney tried to snap a few photos of the dogs, but Clo wouldn't look at her and kept burrowing deeper into the sleeping bag.

"None of your subjects are cooperating," David said.

"Guess not," Courtney said. "That's okay."

"What are your parents going to do about their house?" Jake asked.

"Well, my dad's sick. And they flooded once already awhile back. They said then that they were leaving if it ever happened again. And now it happened again. My father thinks they should just give that land out by the lake back to the lake. That they never should have built on it."

"Or they could just go up twelve feet," I said. "I mean, not them. But somebody in the future. I like nature, but I don't want to give the house back to it. Why doesn't everybody in the rest of the country give their houses back to nature?"

"Hey, don't tell me," David said. "I'm just the messenger."

"I'm just saying, be careful when you start down that road. Then you definitely have to give your dry house back to nature because of the Mississippi River levees. And everyone on the coast for three miles all the way around the country should give their buildings back to nature, too."

David smiled. "Maybe I will."

"Right," I said.

As Courtney crouched on her knees and tried to move the sleeping bag away from the dogs' faces, I felt a creep of warm-house resentment. Courtney and David were living a closer-to-normal life, picking up their cameras and moving on. After months of front-yard confessional, I didn't feel like the same person I had once been. I was wondering if I would ever again. The only way for us to possibly get our time back would be to leave town completely, and it felt like that wouldn't work, either. Even dumping a flooded house was work.

"Do you know you can see the stars here now?" I said. "It's like Mississippi."

"Yeah," Courtney said. "We saw them out by David's parents' house."

"We saw a hawk around the corner on Banks Street on a fence," Jake said. "An actual hawk. Just sitting there."

Jake forged an alliance with Pastor Jim, the freelance minister with the lecherous wolf tattoo. When he was a kid forty years ago in Mid-City, Pastor Jim and his brother used to pilfer cartons of milk from outside a corner store a block away. Now he owned flooded rental properties in Mid-City and another neighborhood. Just like an occasional returning older neighbor friendlily confessed that she begrudged me my second story and my dregs of youth and my twenty-nine-year-old Jake, occasionally I begrudged Pastor Jim his unflooded home across the lake.

Dealing with New Orleans City Hall could be convoluted even before the flood. Pastor Jim felt we should marshal the troops.

"You going to be all right here by yourself if I take Jake downtown?" Pastor Jim said, glancing up and down the deserted street. "I mean I guess you stay here at night and all."

"I've got these vicious dogs," I said.

Pastor Jim cracked a smile. He had a salt-and-pepper crew cut and a leftover milk-stealing grin.

Buster and Clo and I were sitting on garbage bags on the broken front porch. Clo rested her head in my lap, her red cape covering her like a blanket. When we moved back into the flooded house, Clo started shivering all the time. Tanio had mailed Clo a snazzy red cape from California.

With her upturned red collar, Clo paraded through disasterland looking smashing. When I walked down the middle of the street to avoid the garbage piles, Buster would drag behind sniffing horrors. But Clo trotted slightly ahead, surveying the neighborhood like a visiting diplomat. People on porches in mold masks would sometimes pull down their masks, smile, and wave. Clo's disaster parade reminded me of Clo's 1997 tinsel spaceman costume for the Mystick Krewe of Barkus parade. Clo's red cape brought back a brief flash of normal New Orleans.

"Yeah, these dogs are serious. Man, I'd think twice if I saw you up here with them. That one especially," he said, thumbing toward Clo resting under her cape.

Neither dog stirred. They had just paraded and they were beat.

"You're really not going to be scared with us gone?" Pastor Jim asked.

"I'm going to work inside. I'm fine, thanks. I'm too busy to be scared. I like to save that for late at night."

"I bet," Pastor Jim said. "My wife would freak."

Pastor Jim had been shocked to learn we were now sleeping there, but also relieved. Us staying there upped his odds of not having his properties stripped. People who wanted to try to fix their houses liked to have at least one other neighbor on the same block fixing his house. It felt like shareholders spreading the risk, but it was more like roulette. Out of twenty houses on our block, it looked like three so far were betting our chips.

"I told Jake two is better than one," Pastor Jim said. "We can get the real information and make them have to deal with us. They're either giving permits or they're not. I don't see how they can put people off for six months of meetings. If they change some rule about elevation or something later, I want to have my permit in my hand. I'll say y'all are the ones who gave me permission to rebuild in the first place!"

"I don't even see what we need permits for," I said. "I can't imagine them coming to check on anything. They can't even get all the boats and cars hauled off."

"That's the reason. So they don't come back at you later with a technicality after you spent all that money," Pastor Jim said. "And you'll need inspections when you get to your electrical."

"If they decide you can't rebuild, I don't see how a permit is going to help."

"How could they decide we can't rebuild? We're in the middle of the city. We're not way out in the East! You got the streetcar on Canal. You have to drive through us to get anywhere!"

"I don't know," I said. "Maybe after the meetings they'll decide we're not going to be the middle anymore. Maybe we're going to be, like, the edge."

Pastor Jim frowned. "Nah," he said. "You think?"

"No," I said. "Maybe. I don't know. But we're going to do a bare minimum, I think. Disinfect and roof and electric and a few walls and see what happens."

"By that time you're already in a lot of money."

"I know," I said. "But maybe by then we'll know more about the levees."

"How could they not fix the levees?" Pastor Jim said. "You really believe that?"

"How could they not have had them done right the first time and say they did?" I said.

Pastor Jim gave me a good, long look. "You're a cynical type. I really believe all that is going to work itself out. I have faith."

A lot of people left in town were getting out either their prayer or their ledger book. A guy Jake knew from college radio days told us he planned to turn this disaster into "positive cash flow" by moving out of state, fixing quickly, and charging the new scalp rent within the year to some poor sop back here in New Orleans. I thought he was in denial about how much money he'd have left when his contractor was finished with him and how long that would take. When we got out our ledger book, it did not quite add up the same. All that had been New Orleans could not fit into the unflooded part, sure. But all that had been New Orleans could not afford to pay $1,400 rent, either.

In theory, we could subdivide the house into four apartments that would irritate any neighbor who made the mistake to fix near us. Then we could bail. We could overcharge some contractors or law students or HUD and cram six cars and fourteen people onto our lot even though we had no driveway just because no one would stop us. This did not seem to be the way to build a decent neighborhood. I hoped none of our neighbors were planning to do that to us.

Before the flood, some of our neighbors had been angry with us when we rented out the house to arts-and-crafters who welded out front and sometimes parked a camouflaged station wagon on the sidewalk. There had been rumors of some kind of live performances in our shed. If we wanted to help fix New Orleans, part of that meant being better neighbors than we had been before.

"Here's another thing we should do," Pastor Jim continued. "Get a group rate on these electricians. I'll say, 'Listen here. We got three houses. Give me a price on both my houses and if your price is good enough, my neighbor down the street might have some work for you, too.' "

"Okay," I said. "But I doubt they're going to be hurting for business."

"You just have to know how to deal with these people," Pastor Jim said. "Make them see it your way. When is your insurance coming to tow that van?"

"Good question," I said.

Though I'd only known him a short time, Pastor Jim had already repeatedly preached his gospel of erosion—his belief that most ends could be achieved through sheer wear and tear. Pastor Jim extolled the virtues of making yourself a menace. It sounded exhausting.

"You need to call them again. I don't see why they won't come get that van," Pastor Jim said. "That's going to give you problems when it's time to bring any equipment. That needs to be gone. They paid you out for that?"

"Yep. They were the quickest. Guess how much it was worth?"

"I don't know. I don't want to insult your van but it doesn't look real good . . ."

The white van looked like it had been dipped in convenience-store coffee. It had stopped dripping. But it stunk and made your eyes water if you got too close.

"It's a biohazard," I agreed. "Guess how much?"

"Three thousand dollars?"

"Nope. Guess again."

Since information seemed like power, many of us were now telling near strangers all of our business. Exactly how much our houses had cost, how much mortgage we owed, how many months we could or couldn't go without work to dedicate to fixing a house without going belly-up, how much insurance we had or hadn't gotten—it was all on the table. It was one big citywide financial rap session.

The lack of privacy was weird. My books and clothes and furniture on the street for everyone to peruse had been a little embarrassing. And when a disaster photographer bicycled up to take photos of me on the porch looking stupid in my gas mask and close-ups of my neighbor's family photo and underwear pile, I had flipped him off. But other aspects of the mass disclosure were liberating. Telling everyone your business felt like the heady wave of camaraderie that must grip cult members months before anyone mentioned the trunkful of Dixie cups and cyanide Kool-Aid.

"We got forty-five hundred dollars for the van."

"Not too bad," Pastor Jim said.

"But now they won't come get it."

Pastor Jim shook his head. "You sure you called them?"

"We already did. I mean Jake did. At least ten times different weeks."

He shook his head again and exhaled deeply. "Let me tell you something. I'd call them *every* day. Five times a day. I would burn up their phone lines."

"Our friend Dave might help us drag it if they don't come soon. Then they can go look for it. We can tell them it was stolen."

Pastor Jim shook his head. Sometimes when he came over to borrow our dolly, he could scarcely hide the bemused expression on his face. He thought we were slackers in over our heads, and maybe we were. Probably he thought he could whip us into shape.

"Well, just to play devil's advocate . . . that could be illegal. They paid Jake for the van, so technically it's theirs," Pastor Jim said.

"So," I said.

Pastor Jim laughed. "That's one way to look at it," he said. "But all you need to do is just call at least five times a day. Make them deal with you. I'm surprised one of those bobcats hasn't hit it. But you can't just steal a van from yourself."

"Never mind. We're just going to drag it in front of one of your houses."

"Right," he said. "Sure."

I was sick of adjusters. We spent days for our wind adjuster snapping flood-crime-scene photos and listing what we had left and what Jake had already thrown out. Spatulas, frying pans, shoes, cameras, paintings, bicycles, desks. Other people refused to touch their houses at all until every last adjuster came, ruining any chance at saving their ceilings or floors to preserve a pristine disaster diorama. Adjusters were a weird bunch. Some adjusters were penny-pinching Midwestern maw-maws. Others fancied themselves disaster cowboys.

"Two different adjuster guys tried to recruit Jake. They kept telling him how much money they make storm chasing."

"Some of those guys only work a few months a year," Pastor Jim said.

"We saw one drive up in a Hummer," I said.

Pastor Jim looked impressed. "Maybe y'all should do that.

You're young. Drive around the country living in hotels follow-ing storms. It's probably not just storms. Big fires, earthquakes. See the whole country."

To me that sounded like a lot of eating Moons Over My Hammy at some Denny's with its roof ripped off, watching peo-ple cry.

"No thanks," I said. "Once is plenty."

"I hear that," Pastor Jim said.

Jake opened the front door behind me. "Okay, ready," he said, patting his pockets for his keys. "Shoot. You have a folder. Do you have papers? All my papers flooded. What are you bringing?"

"My papers," Pastor Jim said. "You may not need them to get a permit. Let's just go find out."

Jake skipped down the stairs. He turned around when he got to Pastor Jim's truck. "Hey, don't start the ceiling by yourself," Jake said. "Work on the studs."

"I'm not planning any accidents," I said.

"And go inside. Lock the door," Jake said.

"Let me know how that mold stuff goes," Pastor Jim called. "I don't know which way we're going to go on that."

"We're probably getting a moisture meter if you want to bor-row it."

"A *moisture* meter?" Pastor Jim said. "I don't like the sound of that."

"Bye." I waved.

"Go inside and then we'll leave," Jake said.

"Come on, y'all," I said, herding the dogs. "Inside."

I had been to several mold seminars at the Preservation Re-source Center. Exhausted New Orleanians sat patiently through the LSU Mold Lady's spore PowerPoint, frowning into the mold-can-be-created-but-never-destroyed handouts. Some horsehair plaster zealots had stood up and testified. Consequently, I knew what bleach and rubbing alcohol could and couldn't do, some random facts about bleach's effects on wood tensile strength, and various factoids about non-phosphate disinfectants and borates with moldicide additives. Now it was time to put them all to use.

Another day some out-of-state architects came to preach the good news that people in South Carolina had saved many old houses after Hurricane Hugo and we could, too. Since it was months after the storm, these volunteer architects were shocked to find themselves wandering through a deserted no-man's-land. They were so earnest, I felt kind of bad for them. The bunch of them had come all this way and no one was around to take their pamphlet.

Volunteers were a weird bunch. We had seen a troop of paramilitary animal rescue women storm from a minivan to get a burrito at Dave's reopened restaurant. I had endured Holy Rollers stepping onto my porch to offer me a gallon of water and a mold mask, a good one—an N-95—to listen to a scripture. When I had no stove, one lady had hoisted a jumbo sack of refugee rice onto my porch like my ribs were showing.

But architects we could use. I told the volunteer architects to come by my house and I would show them a classic, gutted double-camelback and they could tell me if I was ruining or saving our floors. That perked them up.

Volunteers wanted to be needed. But it seemed like a lot of them were either too early or too late.

a monster moonwalking

After a month or so of lanterns and candles, an electrician nailed a lone, blue, temp outlet on a stud in our gutted living room. We plugged in an extension cord and minifridge, then strung Christmas lights through the studs, down the hallway, and up the stairs. If you narrowed your eyes the lights fizzed and you could pretend it was the skyline from the old Top of the Mart or the Mermaid Lounge after a balmy night of music.

Some days Jake would put down his tools, dust off, and pick up his camera. He would drive his new, used pickup truck to film something left standing and wrought-ironed to remind people what New Orleans had been for Nola tourism marketing powers-that-be. Some days I would put down my tools, dust off, and go write or produce something that showed the ugly opposite. We were both telling the truth. In this way, we canceled the tiny bleeps either of us sent out into the mediasphere.

I was tired of brushing my teeth with bottled water and spitting into a cup and driving all the way Uptown to shower at the Jewish Community Center. Despite my attempts to be all evolved about it, I had flood issues. The people with time to ponder and oil their abs made me angry. I wanted to knock them off their elliptical machines. Though I was raised Catholic, I had been exposed to a lot of evangelicals in my life, too. I almost could not believe the JCC's no-strings-attached largesse. I half-expected someone to slip into the shower stall next to me and ask if I had accepted Yahweh.

After a few months of camping, the cavalry arrived in the form of a red-haired math teacher who used to cruise Mid-City on an old bike. A few FEMA trailers and neighbors had joined us on our street. Seeing that nothing too bad had happened to us canaries camping in the coal mine, the math teacher wanted to move back into the upstairs of her flooded house. She offered us the little un-flooded place she had been staying in by the fairgrounds.

The little house had purple floors and pink walls and half of a backyard garden and working showers and a little heat. It was heaven. With her offer in hand, Jake called to officially get us off the FEMA trailer list. FEMA said their computer had already bumped him from the list again anyway.

Jake did not want the flood thieves to get all our tools or plumbing. And we didn't want to lose the sublet over the dogs. So Jake and Clo and Buster still spent half their weeknights sleeping upstairs in the flood zone. I felt bad, but not bad enough to camp with them more than once or twice.

Soon a man down our block who knew electricians and car-penters finished slapping his house back together quick. A large family moved in on the other side of his wall. When they lugged their few things into the apartment in garbage bags, we were thrilled. With them, the math teacher, and the occasional FEMA trailer beginning to crop up around us, we could worry less.

No, the handful of neighbors was not near the sixty or so who had inhabited our block before the flood, but more people meant more eyes to keep watch. Keeping watch was exhausting. Former neighbors dropped by to ask us if anyone had fooled with their houses. They demanded answers. *Who dumped those rotten fridges in my driveway? Whose rooster is that jumping on that gutting pile? It's an infection waiting to happen.* We did not always have answers.

Soon a FEMA trailer sprouted in the fixed house's driveway with a teenager who did not go to school. And then we noticed that the fixed apartment full of kids also did not go to school. Instead, a small boy bounced and flipped on a moldy mattress pile on the side of the street. A child too old to be sucking his thumb did and went around looking for hugs. Another was so bored he asked for a hammer to help me rebuild. I did not want any children getting hurt on my construction site. I thanked him and said no.

To pass time, the kids sifted through gutting piles and sometimes skipped around the flood zone without shoes. I talked to their mother and invited them to the neighborhood association barbecue. She had a small tattoo on her forehead and seemed spacey. Sometimes the children seemed to stay alone. One night a neighbor saw a few of the children lighting phone books for fun on abandoned porches. Soon the moldy mattress flipper had a broken leg.

In New Orleans before the storm, some kids hung out on corners and children often watched other children. Over the years, I'd watched friend after friend attempt to alter the lives of various hard-luck kids with little success. These friends had purchased books and school uniforms and bicycles for kids on their blocks. They handed out cash to kids and their adult relatives. They started volunteer art programs. Helen threw a few cotton candy and tea parties. I had tutored and volunteered in the past, but I didn't anymore.

Many New Orleans people did many things to sand the edges off of the rough reality they saw outside their front doors. But kids were still poor. They still went to abysmal schools. Many of their home lives careened up and down. Little ever changed. People argued about whose fault it was. Because kids were suffering in plain sight, the blame and you-should-be-ashamed went round and round until everyone got dizzy. Depending on who you asked, it was the government's fault, history's fault, the parents' fault, the children's fault, your fault, or my fault.

Mom, Jake, and I had spent weeks trying to get state or local social services to help the first forgotten family. Even though the developmentally disabled teen was getting into screaming slap fights with his mentally ill guardian, even though he was wandering into people's houses scavenging, even though a neighbor a block away said the kid was going to get himself shot by a scared returning homeowner, even though they lived in teeming junk-pile squalor, even though we sometimes saw them hiking miles away with moldy stuffed animals strapped to their backs on their way to a Christian food tent, there was nothing anyone would do.

One afternoon two officers ventured in to check the forgotten family's medicine cabinet. They came out shaking their heads. They frowned in the street and sighed deep, exhausted sighs and phoned their staff psychiatrist. They said they had been working long shifts for months and got calls every week about this forgotten family and others like them. Charity Hospital was flooded and there were no psych beds or social workers. They said the big teen was better off living with no water, heat, or electricity in a flooded garbage pile with a mentally ill old woman screaming "Abuser!" and boxing him than locked up with real criminals in OPP. And that's what they had to offer. In a way, the hard-luck kids had it good in comparison.

Into this wonderland, appeared a drug addict with greased-back hair driving a van painted black with house paint. It had Texas plates. He set up shop on our corner whistling as he displayed the stolen bicycles and tools he had for sale.

After a few days of general sleaziness, I noticed him curling his finger a lot, calling over one of the younger hard-luck kids. This child's slightly older brother had already gotten in trouble for breaking into people's backyards and stealing tools and stripping bikes. Now here was a flood sleazeball beckoning the six-year-old across two lanes of disaster-truck traffic.

Their parents weren't around. Many days Jake was off filming or editing and I was pulling nails and sanding and running to the hardware store with some guy or other. I was the only adult around to notice this budding friendship. At the very best, the flood sleazeball was trying to get the little boy to work for him. At the very worst, I didn't know. We had had a few squatters turning up. He seemed like one.

One afternoon, the disaster hobo had the supposed-to-be-first-grader from the hard-luck family over at his stolen junkpile. My legs started walking over there. All of a sudden, I was on Banks Street pointing my hammer like some screamer on *The Jerry Springer Show*. It was embarrassing.

"Whatever you're doing, you're not going to do that here," I said.

"Lady, I'm here rebuilding this town," he said.

"You're not going to set up shop on this sidewalk every day. I know you didn't stay in that house before. I doubt you're supposed to be there now."

"Lady, is that any way to treat someone here to help your city?"

The supposed-to-be-first-grader rocked back and forth on his oversized bike. His eyes got big.

"Around here, grown men don't spend all day calling over other people's kids. When his dad gets back, he's not going to appreciate it."

The little boy grinned. He was enjoying the fuss.

"Lady, I love kids. Lady, I resent the suggestion. A man can have a garage sale."

"And someone can call the cops and say someone who doesn't live here is fencing stolen shit on a corner he doesn't belong on and spending all day long calling over little kids."

"Be my guest," he said.

"I will," I said, and walked across the street to do just that.

The little boy trailed me, saying, "Hey. Hey. He told me something about some bikes."

"I know," I said. "Let's not talk to him anymore, okay? Let's ignore him when he calls you. That's not a nice man."

Sometime in the midst of the cops and the little kid, the kids' dad came home. He walked over with his eyes burning. I couldn't tell who he hated more—me or the drug addict. He walked up to the guy.

"You're a grown man," he said. "Stop talking to my kids."

Jake yelled at me when he got home. He thought the man with the house-painted van looked like Greyhound stations and knives. Like Florida panhandle trash even though he had Texas plates.

"Just fix the house," he said. "You can't make parents not leave kids home alone. Cops drive by and see them playing in the garbage all the time. You can't make anybody care they're not in school."

"But I don't have to sit around and watch Black Van do something to them," I said.

"I don't know," Jake said.

But just when project Mayberry wasn't going so well, little miracles happened. I found a horseshoe in the wall and, in the ceiling, two ancient and tiny button-up women's shoes. One day some blond, Southern women, some Ladies of Garbage, strapped on work gloves over their manicures and donned orange vests to pick up flood garbage on a street near us.

Other miracles included the appearance of a plumber. Just as we had been searching without luck, a long-haired, mustached plumber saw us outside and parked his van. He told us he had spent some of his best years in our house. He showed us where he used to grow pot on our back balcony in the early eighties and where he had rigged an outdoor summer shower. He shed some light on the mystery of the barbed-wire fence between our neighbor's house and ours.

He had stopped by to see if the antique O'Keefe & Merritt stove he had restored and left in our kitchen had survived the flood. It was a fine stove with a double oven, curved Art Deco back with built-in salt and pepper shakers, and a griddle in the middle. We loved that stove, we told him. I loved that stove, he said. My wife loved that stove. We all loved that stove and now it was rusted, flooded, and gone.

He thought I could have saved it. I told him I had cleaned and oiled it for months and looked the insulation up on the Internet and tried, but it rusted from the bottom anyway. He gave me a talking to—I hadn't tried hard enough. A few days later he brought another plumber, his old housemate, by. The old housemate went room to room pointing, "I fucked right there, I fucked right there, and I fucked right there." They said they would help us.

Near us people had bigger miracles. In a gutted house on the next block where a man lived upstairs with a lantern, one night when Jake and I walked the dogs by, he invited us to lay our hands on the side of his home. He said that two roofers had just fallen two stories off the top of it, bounced on the flood-wrecked grass, and survived. Groups of Hispanic workers streamed by all day and pressed their palms to his wall. He said we should touch his ruined house because it was blessed.

Mardi Gras itself had been a miracle. It was like a family reunion. Nationwide shooshing over whether we were spoiled decadents made me wonder if it was wrong for me to do what I had done since I was a child. Exhausted and eager to wave our arms like we used to, I had put on my bead skirt, and Jake and I and our neuroscientist-turned-Sheetrocker friend, Jeff, put down our drills and headed to some parades and the Quarter. We laughed and swung our feet and consorted with drag queens and felt somewhat like ourselves again.

Though I was right where I had always been, sometimes in the flood zone I felt disappeared. I spent most of my time working on the house. I used to read a book a week. Now in my spare time I researched and read construction books, Googled arcane arguments about insulation or wiring, and dropped in on strangers to determine exactly how they were bracing something. I shadowed Keith, Pastor Jim's Rasta carpenter, to pick up floating techniques. All the problems and constant labor that had pulled Jake's amp plug also crowded out much of our old lives, projects, and friends. I was hoping New Orleans was not toxic like everyone said.

Displaced friends had tried to help from afar. From South Carolina, Helen had sent sublet leads, advice, and complaints. She had sent a man to our house who she was worried was depressed from camping out alone in Mid-City. She wanted me to talk with him. I wasn't sure what to say. When he bicycled out of a plaster dust cloud to my front steps, I conjured some great obviousness: *Go out of town if you possibly can.* We were all a little lost.

Helen and Paul also sent art that reminded me of better days. Back around Halloween, Helen had sent an animation scored with a great Paul song. She drew a cartoon monster moonwalking out of the flooded dollhouse kitchen looming over my backyard. Helen's goofy green monster and Paul's monster ditty made me feel better. It gave me another picture to superimpose over some of what I had seen. When I sat on their backyard glider in my yard, instead of remembering that dollhouse kitchen's owner crying with her head in her hands on her back stoop, I could look up and see Helen's jiggly green moonwalking monster. He liked his suddenly al fresco table, and he was enjoying a spot of tea.

in bloom

Before the flood, Mom and I had strolled all over New Orleans checking out people's gardens—courtyard gardens, moonlight gardens, formal gardens, cottage gardens, some random dude with cotton bolls or papaya trees lining his front walk. Curtains of jasmine draped from cables off telephone poles. We found lily pads the size of frying pans at City Park and peeked over my friends' fences to see what was growing. Mom would thump heavy stalks of hanging bananas in my backyard. "It's that swamp soil," she said.

One year when my backyard felt tiny, I planted a satellite garden at the Green Project in Mid-City—the old Gold Seal Dairy converted to a salvaged building materials warehouse with community garden plots in the back. There in the wet New Orleans heat grizzled old construction men, non-profiteers, and kitchen-haircut anarchists talked barge board and slate. When Mom came by, I would point out an elderly lady who pulled rusty nails out of recycled lumber for hours.

"Don't look now," I'd say. "But she can go like that all day."

"Good for her," Mom said.

But the first garden Mom and I ever shared was a grief garden. A short time after my father died, Mom got a thousand longleaf pine and fir tree saplings. She loaded four or five of us kids into her station wagon and hauled us out to the settlement to work on our hands and knees. Mom was in her late thirties. I was in grade school. Lori, a year younger, was an enthusiastic but hyper junior farmer. We had to keep an eye out so she did not sprint out past the fields into the creek. She kept pulling my digging arm out of its planting hole.

"My hands are cold," I whined. "My hands are freezing off! None of my friends have to plant trees."

"La dee dee," Mom replied. "You kids are some kind of spoiled. You think this is something? What do you think I did when I was your age? You get to watch cartoons before school. See that barn?"

"I help Lori get dressed," I protested.

"And I appreciate it," Mom said.

Mom's working in the fields was a fact, I knew. There was the weathered wood farmhouse, the barn, the depressing picker sheds, the tractor that looked like it belonged in a black-and-white movie, and the fields. But still I found it hard to picture miniature Mom toddling through the rows with her head in a Magyar kerchief holding her wooden berry basket.

To me Grandpa was the old farmer and Mom was the city woman. Grandpa was the one who cranked sausage into revolting intestine balloons at our dining room table. He showed up at our house holding brown paper grocery bags of corn, plums, tomatoes, green peppers, cucumbers, and whatever else he grew. Grandpa was the living past, an old Hungarian cuss, half jovial, half crotchety. Any minute he was liable to appear on his porch, spot us all on our knees planting, and yell *kutya szar!* which meant *dog shit.* He knew we kids would all laugh and know what that meant in Hungarian.

Back then I didn't understand why we were planting so many trees. We were just reseeding. A mother left with five kids alone was trying to hand-plow a new field. It's just us now. Let's plant these trees. That's what New Orleans felt like, too.

Spring warmed the ground. Someone had told me about seeing lemons bobbing down the street during the flood. Now things that floated in on the flood began to sprout. On our walks, Clo and Buster sniffed out cucumber vines and tiny cherry tomato plants growing crowded against sidewalks. A few sunflowers suddenly waved from between piles of garbage. Two cacti struggled on at the bottom of a telephone pole in a tiny bit of their remaining sand. I came back with my work gloves and Jake's truck and hauled the survivors home.

People had looked at the towering dead stands of magnolias still waiting to be cut down around our neighborhood and assumed the worst. Since the brackish lake had washed through, they said our soil had turned to salt. All the wild sprouting proved them wrong.

It was true that my worms were gone. Digging in the backyard I had noticed the soil was compacted and all the worms had disappeared. In the front yard, the disaster–garbage truck claws had scooped away most of our dirt along with the debris. Where plants and soil had been now stood a flattened hard moat of plaster chunks, broken glass, and nails.

After months of ugliness, I really needed something green. I phoned Mom to see if she had extra plants.

"What's going on in your yard?" I said.

"Why? You coming over?" she asked.

"I wanted to see if you had any plants that need dividing," I said. "I'm sick of looking at that moat. It's disgusting. It keeps filling up with garbage."

"Then where are you going to put all your garbage?" she said.

"Oh, garbage, garbage, garbage," I said. "You and Jake."

Mom was an occasional but key member of my Shop Vaccing

crew. She also liked to check for health and safety code violations. Recently she had requested I buy or borrow a super magnet so we could attract nails throughout the house and yard. She thought we could spare ourselves some of the frequent flat tires by sweeping this magnet when I walked the dogs up and down my street.

"I'm telling you that you're not close to finished with that garbage," Mom said. "Listen to Jake."

"Jake thinks it's a bad idea. I'm going to move our cars and then start bagging the junk that we can and putting the rest on the edge of the street. And start going to the dump."

"That might not be practical," Mom said.

"I can't look at this garbage for another year! Disaster guys threw their chuckwagon leftovers in it and a rat came out. Jake had to throw a rock. It wouldn't back down. Do you want me to go crazy?"

I was beginning to realize that back in the fall I had been in denial. I had told quite a few people that we could get back to seminormal in six to eight months. Now six to eight months had passed. We now had a roof and some wiring but only that same downstairs temp outlet. No real electricity or overhead lights. We weren't even half-finished.

Since some of our neighbors were rebuilding and some of Jake's work seemed to be returning, we wanted to at least get the lights on and hang and float the Sheetrock. But looming over us was the backyard dollhouse with its back wall still missing and another just like it on our corner. Many other houses on our street and all across town had ragged curtains with mold spores blooming in their windows. Through thousands of smudged windows gloomy dioramas of 2005 persisted. If that was all I had to look at for the next year, it would undo me.

"You're not going to go crazy," Mom said. "That's ridiculous."

"It's possible," I said. "I feel weird."

"I'm sure you do. It's been a lot of changes for everybody."

"Well Jake is acting weird. He might go crazy."

"Weird how?" Mom wanted to know.

"Like he might get into a fight with somebody. After that electrician robbed us, he kept saying he felt like punching somebody in the face."

"*Jake?*" Mom said. "The Jake I know?"

"Yes."

Mom sighed. "Well, he's just blowing off steam."

"I don't know. He didn't used to blow off steam like that. I was actually scared he was going to fight the electrician. He kept calling him and yelling at him even after it was pointless."

"*I'd* be mad at that," Mom said.

"Yeah, but take the hit, move on. He robbed us. Oh well. I mean, not *oh well*, but oh well."

Sometimes Disaster Jake came in handy. Like when the other electricians let our dogs out and we had to search for hours in and out and between the abandoned houses as night fell. It was lonesome and spooky and I was glad Disaster Jake was there. But sometimes I wondered if a switch had been flipped.

When Disaster Jake chewed the fat with Pastor Jim and other neighbor men, he downed his water in one long gulp. He said things like *property value*. He told the dogs to shut up, and he sounded like he meant it. And Disaster Jake sometimes shot me the worst looks. If he didn't like my worldview some days, Disaster Jake said, "You need to take those hippie goggles off of your face."

Hearing Disaster Jake talk sometimes I thought, You know what, Disaster Jake, you're an asshole. Let regular Jake go. Disaster Jake was not real Jake and I didn't want him interfering with my garden.

"Jake's just been a jerk lately," I said. "That's all I'm saying."

"Well, sometimes when I'm over there, you're bossy," Mom said. "You know I'm going to be honest. You're both under a lot of stress. But some days you're something terrible. I don't know how you two aren't killing each other."

"I'm not going around saying I'm going to punch somebody!" I said. "I'm not the one sitting around with the carpenter shooting out shed windows."

"Well, that's not safe. That'll put glass all over your yard."

"That's not the point. It's getting like a disaster fraternity or something over here. Or a hunting camp. Or an oil rig."

"Or a construction site," Mom said.

"Yeah," I said. "It's obnoxious."

"Well, I'm sorry. What did you think it was going to be? This, too, shall pass. Do you want me to bring you some túrós galuska or gumbo or garbage bags or anything when I come?"

"No. Just bring me your extra plants."

People usually landscape last, but I didn't want to wait for however long normal took to reseed my garden. I was also going to replant the pit bull Jesus and Virgin Mary grotto across the street. Soon our block would have a mini-oasis of green. Someone had stolen my pit bull Jesus, and I had nothing bright out there to appeal to when I was pulling glass out of the legally blind man's foot down the street. Jake had warned me that someone would take pit bull Jesus if I put him out to save him from our swinging hammers. He was right. I came out one morning and the hurricane miracle was over. Flooded Mary was alone.

I had reason to believe the thief was Chris, our old punk curmudgeon friend who had helped us in the disaster line. Once he left the disaster line, Chris scootered around the flood zone snapping digital photos like that would save something. He was on a crusade to archive all the old, hand-painted po-boy signs on collapsing corner store buildings before they fell. I noticed when he had scooted up our street to visit one day, he had admired pit bull Jesus and the hurricane miracle a little too much. Maybe Chris had snuck back, lifted the dreadlocked savior by his outstretched

arms, and pit bull Jesus had surfed away on the floorboard of his
Vespa. Now pit bull Jesus was off gallivanting on the Isle of Denial and we were stuck.

As soon as I got the crepe myrtle and the cassia and the irises
and Mom's begonias planted, the orange-vesters started angling
their bobcats around it. Clo and Buster lolled in the soft mulch.
Jake said he might want a Japanese magnolia some day. I was surprised what an impact a few struggling plants could make.

To me my new plants didn't look that great. It was a skinny
ghost of my former garden. But old couples would honk and point
and smile and wave. Men and women stopped their cars, rolled
down windows usually shut against the drywall dust breeze, and
called out tearfully from behind the wheel. "It's beautiful!" they
said.

"Domo arigato Mr. Roboto . . . Himitsu wo shiri tai!"
The new carpenter I had found while walking the dogs was
rocking it out. Between the splitting wood and Styx blaring from
Rich's yellow construction boom box, I could barely hear any
thing he said. Rich crowbarred up another floorboard. Standing
on the dirt below with his blond crew cut, he looked cut off at the
waist like a Marine in a foxhole.

I gazed into the gaping hole in our living room floor. I could
see the rusty pipes and black dirt below. I hated that hole. The dirt
under the house seemed dirtier since the flood and I didn't like
looking at it. Also we had rats, which we'd never had before. But
Jake kept saying no, they weren't *rat* rats, just "big mice." Whatever they were we would find their jumbo droppings scattered all
over downstairs. I was also leery of the attic. An electrician had
come out upset.

"I wouldn't go in there if I were you," he said. "They're crawl-
ing all over each other."

A band of roaches had scurried up to escape the water and

started a hive and, over months, well, grew. We called a pest man and then the roaches rained a few droplets at a time for a week through the gutted ceiling. They were supposedly gone now, but still.

"You're wondering who I am . . . secret secret I've got a secret . . . machine or mannequin?"

"One thing I hope this patch we're doing doesn't wind up looking like is a giant trap door," I said.

"Gotcha gotcha," Rich said, ripping up another floorboard. "We're going to . . ."

"With parts made in Japan . . . secret secret I've got a secret . . ."

"Huh?" I called.

"Gotcha gotcha," he repeated louder. "We'll stagger it!"

"Oh. All right." I nodded and smiled.

Rich was in his late twenties and wore wraparound sunglasses. *Gotcha, gotcha* is how he tended to greet most comments from me, his weird female assistant. When he wasn't rocking, he talked and I listened. From our short time together, I learned a lot about him. He was a former EMT and an ardent fan of police and police work. He was also taking scuba-diving classes because he might change careers to be one of those guys who scraped barnacles from the bottom of boats. Divers got to swim all day. They made good money. Other construction guys weren't always letting them down.

"Can you find me four more pieces? This one's split and this one's no good. Oh and Cheryl? The longer the better. You'll thank me in the end. Trust me. And when you bring them down I want you to pop the nails out like this," he said.

He held up a floorboard and hammered the rusted, square nail out backward with one pop. Sometimes Rich's demos were pure bragging.

"I'll try," I said.

I had found Rich while walking Clo and Buster and checking out houses people were gutting and working on. Many of the neighbors who had touched their houses at all were, like Jake and me, pounding on it themselves with whatever little help they could find. A lucky few had relatives in the construction business or a crew of Brazilians. A slew of shady guys cruised brand-new pickup trucks slowly around the big debris piles in our neighborhood making dubious promises or tacking We Buy Flooded Houses signs high up on telephone poles. When they saw me working, they often jumped out and offered big fish stories, hot-off-the press business cards, and outlandish estimates.

The phone books still didn't work well since most everyone in them was gone, so whenever I came upon someone who didn't look like a carnie, I'd stop and say, "Hey, you framed that window? That looks great! Can I get your number?" Often I implied that our disaster was a better disaster, a more fun disaster—one that came with free assistants and hilarious dogs.

Walking the dogs one day, I came upon Rich reframing someone's back wall and it had looked straight when he finished. He had gotten off his ladder and petted both basset hounds while I subjected him to my interrogation. Did he do his own work or did he sometimes pick up guys slouching on the corner whose construction skills would possibly finish off what the wind and water had not? Yes, he swung his own hammer. He did not like strangers breaking his tools. What's more, he was from New Orleans. He looked like he had showered that very morning. I felt like I'd won the lottery.

I picked my way through the lumber and tools and climbed the stairs to get the wood he needed. Jake was disassembling a closet in the attic that had been constructed of leftover heart pine floorboards. Since it was above the floodline and since most salvage yards in New Orleans had gone under, the closet wall was a lucky stash. Jake peeked out of the miniature attic door. Black soot smeared his face and glasses like a coal miner.

"Here, take these," he said, handing me an armload of floor-boards.

"We need more. Some of the ones we have are split and one's warped," I said.

"What? These are almost the last ones!"

"Maybe you should pull some out of the floor," I suggested.

"There's only a few feet of it. If I pull it we'll fall through the ceiling when we walk in here."

"Well, just get what you can," I said.

"Is he sure he doesn't have enough?"

"The hole's getting a little bigger," I admitted.

Jake sighed. Jake sighed all the time lately. Big, raging, fed-up sighs. Sometimes I told him he better watch out or he would burst a vein.

"Is he making it worse than it was?" Jake asked. "I told him I just wanted it patched neatly."

"Depends on your definition of *was*," I said.

"Shut up," Jake said.

Besides Jake and I, Rich had two other guys with him to help pull apart the rotted front porch that day—a young guy with a shaved head and smudgy neck tattoos and another older guy with a frown and a dirty-blond ponytail. That was today's crew.

"Wassup?" they had asked as they nodded to me that morning.

"Nice to meet you," I'd said.

Jake and I trudged downstairs with an armload of floorboards each, ready to do battle with the hole. It was strangely silent in the front of the house. Had the rock of New Orleans gone off the air? Rich and the other two guys all stood with their arms dangling at their sides at the half-open front door, ears cocked and listening. I put down my boards.

"Did y'all just hear that?" Rich said.

"What?" I asked.

"What?" Jake repeated.

Rich held a finger to his lips, peered out the front door, and then shut it fast.

"Shit," he said.

"What?" I said.

"You're not going to believe it."

"What?" I said.

"Those kids shot somebody!" Neck Tattoo blurted.

"Maybe they just shot off some firecrackers," I said dumbly.

Neck Tattoo looked at me like I was crazy. "That little dread-lock kid shot that other kid!" he said. "I saw the gun and came in here!"

I felt sick.

Rich and the two guys kept taking turns going to the front door, stepping out onto the porch, and ducking back in.

"I'm telling you he shot him! He shot him," Neck Tattoo said again. "I saw the blood coming out his fuckin' leg."

"Y'all shut the door then," I said. "Stop going outside! You want to get shot by a kid?"

I looked at Jake. Should we go to the back of the house or lie down on the floor? Was that necessary? It seemed extreme, like a tornado drill, yet that was what you were supposed to do.

"Shit, my gun's in the truck," Rich said. "I knew I should've brought it in. I'm going to get my gun."

Ponytail went out on the porch and then stepped back in. "Now they're beating the shit out of the other kid!"

I went to the front door. Hoping not to catch a stray bullet, like an idiot I peeked out. I saw three electricians watching in shock from the house on the corner. An old man down the street walked into his gutted house and firmly shut the door. I didn't see the gun. A few houses down, I saw one of the hard-luck kids. Teenagers twice his size were holding him by his dreadlocks and kicking him in the face as his head snapped and bled. I wanted to yell *stop*.

But I didn't. And no one else did either because a kid had already shot someone. My hands started to shake. Someone yanked me back inside.

"I'm getting my gun," Rich said again.

"Rich, please don't go get your gun and please don't go out there," I said. "Just call the police."

"I already am," somebody, I think it was Jake, said.

When the police and detectives arrived, the kids were hiding in their apartment with their gun. At first the detectives milled around, not knocking on the door. The kid who was shot had limped off bleeding. The police returned to their squad cars to leave, but the electricians who had been hiding in a house across the street yelled out at the officers to do their jobs and knock on that damn door. Soon a gray-haired man from a few blocks away walked over.

"I heard the sirens and I looked in my alley and I saw this kid bleeding!" he said. "Y'all working on your house?"

"Trying," I said.

"Trying is right. Me, too," he said. "This is some shit."

"Yeah," Jake said.

disaster season

In the midst of August hurricane season dread, Helen e-mailed that she was moving back and coming over. In addition, I better put down my hammer and come to her Home Movies show. I was surprised and not surprised. She had written that she was homesick.

Whether to return home to New Orleans was a huge decision. Musician friends who had moved to Brooklyn and elsewhere, now miserable, called or came to town, dropping by to talk. They wanted to know if New Orleans was ready for them yet. They always asked, "How is it *really*?"

People enjoyed regular lives, probably even had fun, in other parts of town. But we would tell these ex-New Orleanians that our lives were not the same. I never knew what any one friend was waiting to hear. There were no guarantees and I never knew what to say. We had moved back from our last sublet into our upstairs again before our overhead lights were turned on. Once we finally passed inspection, I was almost too exhausted to celebrate.

We never made it to the Home Movies show. On a road trip to New Orleans, Jake's stepsister's car spun off the road, killing her. I didn't believe in curses, but, come on, was New Orleans a Bermuda Triangle? Was New Orleans cursed? In the face of Jenny's death, for the first time in a year, pumping station and street flood worries, levee speculation, construction and bureaucratic and work problems slammed to a halt. Jenny was Jack's little girl and bug-collecting buddy all grown up—a PhD student and an ex–Peace Corps gal. We went to Florida to help.

Helen wrote to me about her thoughts on tragedy piled upon tragedy. She thought that the whole hurricane year was about anything, anywhere happening to change your whole life. I agreed. In New Orleans all year I had witnessed repeat instances of this phenomenon—house fire upon flood upon suicide upon heart attack upon cancer upon freak tree limb–cutting electrocution upon getting gassed from mixing cleaning supplies with bleach trying to clean your rotted fridge. Turned out that kind of thing was not for bad made-for-TV movies only. It was real.

Crazy, crazy stuff happened to old neighbors and other flooded people every day. All the bad stuff that was destined to happen in life anyway got piled on top of the extra debris that all the lucky-to-be-alive flooded people were still trying to crawl out from under. Yet somehow the idea of people reeling from punch after punch and staggering up may-I-please-have-another had seemed dreadful and far-fetched. After Jenny's wreck, it just seemed dreadfully common.

I picked up some platitudes somewhere along the way, very possibly during nine years of kiddie catechism; they had somehow sunken in. Along with *Just offer it up*, there was *God won't give you more than you can handle*. Oh crap. It was so very possibly not true. How had I missed that? I hoped Jake would be okay.

Chapter 18

fall again

Tanio rolled up to the curb next to our construction garbage pile in a fat white Chrysler that looked like a Rolls-Royce. It was the fall of the year after the flood. Tanio had not seen his co-dog, Clo, since before the mess began. Tanio's last car was a Toyota that flooded in the May '95 flood in New Orleans. Somehow the car kept running well enough to take Tanio to Oakland. He kept driving it for years until the brakes finally rusted through and locked up on the interstate. The faux Rolls was pearlier than the three FEMA trailers on our block. Tanio saw me on my new porch, shaking my head and laughing. He hopped out.

"Hey, Hef," I said. "You're looking cash money."

Tanio buffed his nails on his Robotron T-shirt and peered over his thick glasses. That was his Player face. He posed next to his ride.

"I asked for a compact," he said.

Tanio had told us on the phone recently about meeting some gaming old-timers who had taught him to restore classic arcade games. I hoped he was not going to talk about arcade motherboards and "discharging the second anode" a lot.

"It looks crazy around here," he said. "You told me. Dad told me. Still. What the hell?"

I had not seen Tanio's dad since after the storm when we had swatted through a fly cloud to find him staring into the black

depths of his Garden District swimming pool. He was now planning on selling his unflooded home and leaving New Orleans for
good. Since Tanio's stepmother's business had flooded, she had already left for a new job on Long Island. His dad was flying in and
out of town juggling his research work, New Orleans, and their
new life. He had become one of those post-Katrina commuters.

"It actually looks unbelievably better than it looked a year
ago," I said. "And a lot better than six months ago. There were
ferrets dried to cages on the curb."

"Don't tell me that," Tanio said.

"Sorry. There are people in a few trailers and a few houses
besides us now. Not many. But it was a lot more garbage *and* less
people."

"If you say so. There's still a lot of garbage," Tanio said.

"Just don't count the piles."

"I went to the marina with Dad. Saw Lakeview. Messed up. It's
good you talked my friend out of buying a house here."

A Goth video game artist Tanio knew had said she wanted to
buy a flooded investment property to help New Orleans. My tales
of thousands of New Orleanians rebuilding with their own hands
while various government entities and flood hoboes kicked them
in the shins or jumped them from behind with a headlock had
alarmed her.

"I didn't talk her out of it," I said. "I just told her the truth. She
thought you could buy something and rent it or flip it and never
be here and some magic honest contractor would appear to do
her bidding. That's not what's going on."

Before the storm, people from California had bought houses
here to use for JazzFest for a few years and then rented them to
New Orleans people for more than local wages paid. I wasn't
against commerce, but I failed to see how more vacation houses
or scalping, out-of-town landlords would help save New Orleans.
I didn't want to live in vacation-house New Orleans with no New

Orleans or Louisiana people. It wouldn't be New Orleans. If the city was going in that direction, I could move anywhere in the world and save myself the rebuilding grief. I wanted back the best parts of the New Orleans that I knew. In that New Orleans, musicians, waiters and waitresses, artists, writers, teachers, and all manner of regular people could afford to rent or own a house.

I pointed to a house down the street where a small palm tree still harboring a Home Depot tag stood next to some abandoned houses and a gutting pile.

"See that house?" I said. "Our friend Ben, this British guy, this musician, used to live there. Now these people from Georgia bought it for a Mardi Gras and JazzFest house. You know how they're getting it done? They bring in their own crew. He's a swimming pool contractor."

"I wouldn't want to vacation on your street," Tanio said.

"Ouch," I said. "Looks like you already are. Aren't you spending the night?"

"Oh yeah." Tanio smiled. "That. I want to spend at least one night with Clo, but I'll probably stay at Dad's mostly."

The kid who had been occasionally dealing drugs out of a FEMA trailer was hanging on the porch of a flooded and abandoned house down the street with his buddies, eyeing us. One day one of the friends, the craziest one, had showed me the gun in his waistband. I used to say hi but now I ignored them. That way the baby-bully would not get the pleasure of grabbing his crotch or patting a gun in his waistband at me. In a weird way, it kind of worked. A détente of sorts reigned.

Construction and disaster workers were the kids' customers, so the business kicked up after work in the afternoons. The teens hid the drugs between the houses and thought no one knew or cared. I wanted to know who were the adult bosses of these kids.

What is up with your block? When I walked the dogs lately, this is what I would hear. Or *Looks like you got a little problem.* Like the drug-dealing kids were my own, like I could point a magic wand and make some man not bring them drugs or make functional parents appear. People from blocks away would call the police when they happened down my street and witnessed the drug dealing. These same folks stood on their paint-spattered front steps and cursed and vowed. *I'm not ruining my nerves and pocketbook to fix my house just to let some punks come along and ruin everything.*

I hated the drug war. I didn't like the government keeping the profit margins artificially high so that the prohibition runners recruited kids into shooting each other over their tiny take in our neighborhoods. I thought the government should sell drugs affordably to adults and let the addiction chips fall where they may. When I talked about my government dispensary, Mom thought I was crazy.

A neighbor around the corner had caught young teenagers in a flooded and abandoned shed next door to him smoking crack. Showing them his gun, he told them he would shoot them if they came back. It was sad. The teen drug dealers made Jake livid. Since that other kid shot that other kid awhile back and then the whole family got kicked out and then squatted the JazzFest house and later an RV before finally disappearing, Mayberry was dead.

"I have been vacuuming up a storm to dustproof your room. Also you have Sheetrock in there. Actual walls. Hung but not floated."

"First class. Where's Clo?" Tanio said. "I miss her. Gimmee."

Jake was pulling off his mask in the living room. He had been sanding upstairs. The sanding mask had cartridges and made him look more soldier than surgeon.

"Hey man, looks good down here," Tanio said. "Looks like somebody's doing something."

"We got a few rooms," Jake said. "We're trying."

"Playing any?"

Jake shook his head. Under his glasses, he had rubber mask marks cut into his face.

"Wrong question?" Tanio said.

"I'm slammed. It's all work. House, doc, house, news, some tourist industrial complex. House," Jake said. "Sucks."

"I need to show you my new Mbox. Got your Pro Tools back up?"

"Yeah," Jake said.

Buster came running when he heard Tanio's voice. Clo trotted in behind him, wearing the red cape Tanio had sent.

"Clo! You look even better in real life than you do in the pictures," Tanio said. "I didn't think the cape would fit that well."

"Yeah, it's weirdly perfect. Sweaters don't usually stretch over the long basset rump," I agreed. "She's styling."

Tanio kneeled down and Clo put her paws on his chest and licked his face.

"Clo, Clo, Clo," Tanio said. "You're Red Riding Hood."

"She wears it constantly; it works great. She shivers if I take it off. I think she looks like a diplomat," I said. "Also sometimes Dracula or Gidget. Depends on the angle."

"Is that paint on Buster's ear?" Tanio said.

"They're always dragging their ears in something," Jake said.

"I gave up that battle. I clean it off and they brush up against something again," I said. "Like Clo's rhinestones?"

"Yes, I do. Very glamorous," Tanio said. "Eww, what's this?" Tanio pointed to a bare square in the fur on Clo's crooked basset arm.

"That's where they shaved her for the IV," I said. "I told you about that. Where do you think all your money is going? They x-rayed her and made her throw up for no reason. I told them she doesn't eat pennies! Then it was her kidneys. That vet sucks. We're switching."

"That's terrible. Poor baby," Tanio said. "Hey, Clo. Clo!"

Clo's head was turned as Tanio petted her and she would not look back.

"She can't hear you," I said.

"What?"

"I told you about that," I said.

"You said she could hear a little!"

"Well, she could hear a little. Then she couldn't."

"She was faking it," Jake said.

"Trotting after Buster when he heard something," I said.

"Jesus," Tanio said. "When did this happen?"

"Don't make me feel bad. I already feel like she's been sick so much from us moving a lot and living in this hellhole."

"It's not your fault," Tanio said. "Poor Clo."

"She stopped waking up unless we poked her," Jake said. "But we thought she was tired from the construction keeping her up all day."

"But then the vet said that's normal when they go deaf," I said.

"Clo!" Tanio said. "What the hell is happening to my Clo?"

"She's getting old," I said.

"No she's not," Tanio said. "We can reboot. We can rebuild her. Oh, Clo."

"Well don't get mad at me," I said. "I already feel, like, how could I not notice when my own dog went deaf?"

"I'm not mad," Tanio said.

"She was a good faker. That's how," Jake said.

"Hey, she knows signs," I said.

"You're kidding," Tanio said.

"Watch this." I walked to the other side of the room. "Turn her head toward me," I said.

I made a tumbleweed motion with my hands. Clo trotted over.

"Clo, you're so awesome," Tanio said. "You are even good at being an old lady."

"Don't feel too bad for her," Jake said. "She still has fun."

"She likes to hang Sheetrock with me and Jeff. She stretches out on the Sheetrock pile while I'm measuring and cutting," I said. "Jake thinks the dogs slow down progress."

"They do," Jake said.

"I think they more than make up for it in worker morale. Jeff has been going to Broadview Seafood and getting this plastic bag of, um, I don't know. Like spicy meat. Turkey necks and sausage. They get the leftovers."

"Man they love Jeff and that meatbag," Jake said. "Also the truck. They love riding in the back of the truck."

"They vie for the wind, kind of," I said. "It's funny."

"Clo gets in front of Buster and steals his air," Jake said. "Her ears hit Buster in the face."

"Clo is on the crew. I need to get a picture of Clo in her cape Sheetrocking to send Molly and Bully."

Since Clo had lived in the Bay Area for a while, she had dog friends. Tanio had had big dreams of Clo being one of those work dogs happily hanging around the Ping-Pong table at some video game company. But Clo bolted and went cube to cube ruining it. Grabbing pizza, barking, scattering collectible action figures, sniffing and tipping over programmers' snack-encrusted trash cans—it just did not fly in the game industry. Whenever Tanio got her settled for a while in his cube, someone would make a noise and she would want to trot off and start the party.

Clotilde Robichaux would happily dig a hole next to you while you gardened. She would recline underneath a café table. She would race herself silly cutting figure-eights on the green grass alongside the Mississippi River at the dog levee. But she did not do industrial parks. She would not sit leashed to a pneumatic chair.

"You ready to eat?" Jake said.

"Liuzza's is back open," I said. "You can now get stuffed artichoke and frosty mugs in Mid-City once again."

"Great," Tanio said.

"On the back of their menu is a photo of the restaurant underwater," I said. "Somebody must have complained, though. Liuzza's wrote that if the photo ruins your appetite, tough."

Whenever anyone finished fixing anything, all us resettler types did a little dance. Dance for all the places you ever went to or even just walked by for years. So there had been a dance for Jesuit High School, a dance for the grocery store, a dance for the head shop by the cemetery that started serving iced coffee and tea, and especially a dance for McHardy's Chicken & Fixin' on Broad when it reopened, burned, and then reopened again. It was the same dance you did for the first little boy you heard practicing his trumpet as he walked down the street. It proved it was possible.

"Sounds good. Y'all ready?" Tanio said.

"Pick me up around the corner," I told Jake.

"Gotcha," he said.

Pick-me-up-around-the-corner meant I was ducking out the back, past the storm dollhouse and through a few abandoned alleys, so the drug dealers would think someone was home. When only the dealers were on the block, we sometimes went out the back—especially since we'd had some stuff stolen and found a small burned lumber torch in the yard. We didn't have anything to steal but tools and computer stuff, but mostly I didn't want someone kicking our cracked and flooded door in and letting Buster and Clo out.

I locked the back door and cut through the path through the junk across the dollhouse yard. On the corner, I jumped into the back of Tanio's car.

"That's messed up," Tanio said.

"It's just temporary," I said.

It was a little weird, but I was used to it. And so far it seemed to work.

"When we didn't have hot water, a guy up on Palmyra showed me how to hook a crawfish cooker up to a claw-foot tub," I said. "He had these candles in sand in a bucket in his window. He burned them when he wasn't staying there at night. He didn't have any electricity but he wanted to make it look like someone was home."

"That is messed up," Tanio said. "It is seriously fucked up over here."

"We didn't do any of *that* stuff," Jake said.

When we got out at Liuzza's, Tanio's creamy Chrysler was tilted to one side. He had a flat. I started to laugh

"Shit," he said. "It's not funny."

Tanio looked worried, so I tried to stop.

"You're breaking my record," I said.

Jake cracked up, too. With all the re-roofing and construction, we had been getting flat tires every few weeks. I had held the record for nine in one tire, but then the tire plug guy said some other guy had beat me with twelve. He said someone else would probably beat that, too.

"She had the record," Jake tried to say.

I was choking.

"What is wrong with y'all? Are you high?"

"Are *you* high?" I said. "Why would I be high?"

"You tell me. I don't know. You're both acting freaky. Ducking out of the back of your house and cracking up."

"Everything's just funny some days," I said. "It's okay."

"Well, I'm glad y'all are enjoying yourselves. But this is my rental car," Tanio said, looking around the flood zone. "How am I even going to fix this? There's nowhere to bring it."

"It's okay," I said. "Don't worry about it. Let's just go in and eat. It'll be here, flat, later."

Tanio looked skeptical.

"That's just how it is now," I said. "I try not to get aggravated or too mad until about the tenth bad thing. This is only like my fifth today. Get used to it."

"*You* get used to it," Tanio said.

"I didn't mean it like that. I meant save yourself some grief. Shit goes wrong all day. Every day. For over a year. Everything is booby-trapped. That's how it is. We're used to ten things going wrong in a row. You're on number one."

"Hate to tell you," Jake said, "but you're probably going to get a few more nails while you're visiting."

"Then I'm staying at my dad's," Tanio said. "I'll come visit but I don't want a nail every day."

He looked around the deserted neighborhood. It still smelled musty like the flood. The hospital across the street was empty; it had been since the day the patients were evacuated after the storm.

"There's nothing open but Liuzza's, so I don't see how this is going to get fixed," Tanio said. "I'm trusting you."

"You're good. It's all fine," I said. "Come on, let's go eat."

"I'll get on the phone during dinner," Jake said.

After dinner and the tire patch, Tanio was still on edge. Tanio is an hour-shower-type person and it was chilly. We didn't have air-conditioning or heat and I wondered if he was going to make it through the night. At bedtime, he carried Clo up the stairs. She was too rickety to walk up anymore.

"Holy shit," he said when he walked into his room.

"Come on. It doesn't look *that* bad," I said. "We got your Sheetrock hung back. Sorry it isn't floated or anything. I warned you it was still primitive conditions. We only got overhead lights a few months ago!"

"No, that," Tanio said, pointing to the corner. "Is that thing loaded?"

"Oh, sorry," I said. "I'll move it."

The shotgun was leaning in the corner next to the stand-up bass. Someone had put out a perfectly good, unflooded stand-up bass on the curb. All it needed was the bridge glued back.

"Whose is that?" he said.

"Jake's," I said. "Ours. I don't know. I told you about that."

"Who knows how to shoot it?" he said.

"I did maybe," I said. "But I kind of forgot. Jake remembers."

"Have either of you even shot that thing?"

"No," I admitted. "I think maybe he was going to, but then we got too busy. I know it's stupid. I'll get it out of here."

"Do you need that?" Tanio said.

"You know," I said. "I really don't know anymore."

A few days later, Tanio came back from his dad's carrying a plastic box of electronics tools and a folding card table.

"My dad is upset you don't have a table," Tanio said. "He wants you to have a table. He sent this."

Tanio's dad had come by to see our rebuilding progress and to check out Tanio's arcade game cabinets. Slightly flooded Toobin' and Star Wars machines were now in one of my stairwells. One night Tanio and Michael had hoisted them into Jake's truck and hauled them over. Then Tanio strapped on one of our mold masks and stayed up late on his hands and knees swabbing the insides with rubbing alcohol and bleach. He said he was doing his part to help the recovery.

"Where do you want the table?" Tanio said.

"Thanks. That's sweet," I said. "But we can afford a table, tell your dad."

"Huh," Tanio said. "It's been over a year and my dad comes over and you're sitting on the floor with your laptop and no table. It's weird. All night he kept talking about you sitting on the floor."

"I just want as little furniture as possible until the house is finished. Also maybe I don't feel like buying furniture with the levees not fixed. The storm drains are still all clogged, too."

"People need a table."

"Want to hear my dining room table pulley idea? A friend of mine in the Quarter had this old metal door on chains. He hoists it up to the ceiling and down when he wants to use it. What do you think of that for anti-flood furniture?"

"Good," Tanio said, "but weird."

"Just tell your dad, thank you very much. I'm sorry it's weird. I don't know why I don't have a table. Why don't I have a table? I guess there's too much junk and sawhorses and lumber around. I have post-traumatic garbage disorder or something. I feel like I'm going to freak out if anyone brings any more stuff into this house."

"Oh, like two flooded arcade machines? Those were finds. You're going to thank me when I get Toobin' running. You love tubing. Also it will teach you to avoid obstacles while running other people into them."

Toobin' is a weird game. You float on your innertube trying not to get a flat while tossing beer cans through various levels of hell—eskimo level, devil level, trippy Canals of Mars. The Toobin' buddies, Bif and Jet, have the same mission, haircut, and face. Logs, rocks, coconuts, mines, snakes, thorny bushes, punks, devils, hillbillies, natives, and terrorists try to snare and sink them. Not to mention the big alligator that keeps swimming up to chomp their innertubes.

"I might just like real tubing," I said.

"That's not true," Tanio said. "Don't you want to get to the final super-party? Check this out."

He put his plastic box on the stairs and pulled out the back of the Toobin' controller panel. He had soldered dozens of candy-coated wires to the green inside of a computer keyboard. It was pretty.

"We stayed up pretty late soldering."

"That looks neat," I said. "Do I have to watch you so you don't shock yourself today?"

"No," Tanio said. "I'm just going to finish soldering this on your card table."

Earlier that week, Tanio had wanted to "discharge the second anode" on the flooded arcade game through one of the outlets that had taken us nearly a year to get reconnected; I almost freaked. I explained that it would take months to get an electrician. It was hard for out-of-town people to comprehend these things.

Clo and Buster sat at Tanio's feet at the card table. He melted a few more wires to the back of the controller panel, then stopped and looked up.

"Do you mind if I ask you something?" Tanio said. "What the hell, Cheryl? What are you still doing here? My mother thinks you should leave."

"What?" I said.

"The city might be dying. It looks pretty dead. My dad's going; he's not the only one. A lot of people are going. Maybe you tried but now it's time."

I didn't know what to say.

"Oh Lord," I said. "An ambush."

"You can't be the only ones doing your part."

"We're not," I said. "We know people on almost every block now around here working. You just can't see them. They're not all staying here."

"That may not matter. It will take years to fix the levees if they do it right. Then you're over here ducking out your back door and sitting on the floor in some dust on your laptop. I'm worried."

"I don't want you to worry," I said.

"You know my dad loved New Orleans, but then it was destroyed. A lot of people he knew left. Now his wife is in New York. Leaving New Orleans isn't going to be easy for him. He was heading for retirement. Ready to settle in, sail on his boat, go fishing in Bay St. Louis, make dinner for people. He invested a lot of his life into New Orleans. He had a great life here. He's depressed; he's pissed. He feels like the federal government allowed all he worked for to be washed away."

"I know," I said. "Everybody is. People are worried. Pete keeps e-mailing me that in the Netherlands we have this. In the Netherlands we have that. We're under sea level and the cutting edge of damming and pumping crapology. Blah, blah, blah. Sucks."

Our friend Pete had emigrated. A lot of his dishwashing files and 16-millimeter movies and T-shirts and stuff had flooded in my shed. I had felt bad. But lately, because I was bitter and flooded, I felt he wanted to be an expat pain-in-the-ass about it.

"Good old Pete," Tanio smiled. "What's Pete doing? Washing a Dutch dish?"

"No. Biking a Dutch bike. And writing."

"So Pete's a biking and drainage expert these days?" Tanio said.

"Guess so," I said. "But he's right. These Dutch engineers came here and basically told everybody how they do it there and how to do it correctly here. They said what we have is primitive. They've been doing it since the Middle Ages, so I guess they should know. They had lost towns. Drowned villages."

"That's hopeful," Tanio said. "I guess."

"Now whether or not our government wants to continue to act like it's a mystery wrapped inside an enigma I do not know."

"I just think you should really think about how long this is going to take. And what the consequences are."

"I don't want anybody to worry," I said. "It's not just the house. It's everything. It seems kind of wrong not to stay and help and fix if you can."

Tanio gave me a good, long look. Then he went back to soldering his wires. "I guess I trust you that you're keeping you and Clo safe. But I also want to go on record as saying that I don't think this is necessarily a good idea."

"I hear you," I said.

"Yeah, you hear me, but promise me that you'll really consider that you might need to leave."

"I will. I do consider it. All the time. It's paralyzing."

Tanio flipped the controller panel over and pressed the red buttons. "Y'all can come stay with me for a while. Whatever. I mean the dogs probably can't. But we could work something out with someone temporarily."

"Sometimes I think we might be about to turn a corner."

"Really?" Tanio said. "Maybe."

"But then it seems like the corner runs away."

"That sounds just like the Canal of Mars level. The water is red and aliens spit at you. I think I got this working," Tanio said. "Wanna see?"

Chapter 19

tumbleset

When our second flooded Christmas rolled around, I counted my blessings to keep my mind off how cold our house was. Blessings included the fact that five of twenty houses on our block were occupied. We had walls, even if they were mostly unpainted ones with no trim. I had filthy, unfinished floors, yes, but solid ones without three-foot holes in them. Unlike all the people who did not flood but had to leave town anyway when their jobs disappeared, Jake and I, since we freelance, still had employment. And, though we had both changed, we still had the dogs, sanity, and each other.

I assumed I could wear my new construction hat for a little longer as long as I believed an end was somewhere in sight. Around Christmas, Jake and I went to our friend's annual turducken party. We attempted to be normal people with social lives instead of construction workers who hung out on the front porch grumbling about two-by-four prices with other neighbor-carpenters.

We decided it was time to reinstitute the Christmas we had canceled the year before. I bought a few gifts. I strung the old Christmas lights from our one-temp-outlet days around a silver ladder in one of our few almost-finished rooms. Clo in her red cape and Buster beside her under our brightly lit ladder tree made a fine Christmas e-card. Michael, whose mother had moved off his sofa into her FEMA trailer in front of her gutted house in New

Orleans East, joined us on our card table for makeshift Christmas brunch.

But some things got worse after Tanio's visit that I was glad he was not around to see. A few guys had been shot and killed on nearby blocks, and more shootings rang out across our tiny, depopulated city.

The neighborhood and New Orleans had not been Shangri-La before the flood, but there were not sleazy flood bum workers squatting houses and stealing copper plumbing and fencing stolen stuff. There were not crack addicts blazing pipes on the street and prostitutes in lingerie strolling a block away. Instead of visiting neighbors, I was driving the dogs to City Park most days to walk.

In late December, half a mile away, the owner of a recently opened bar shot and killed a twenty-two-year-old would-be robber who bled to death on the floor while patrons pelted him with bottles and a barstool. A few days prior, a popular local high school band director and brass band drummer was shot and killed while driving his wife and kids down the street. Things seemed unhinged.

One afternoon in early January, I sat down on the edge of the bed to read what I had taken to glumly calling the morning murder report. I opened my laptop and came across a headline that didn't make sense. I tried to read it again but my eyes kept getting stuck.

"Jake!" I yelled.

His footsteps hit the stairs. He rushed in the bedroom, winded.

"Shit," he huffed. "Don't scare me like that. I thought you fell off a ladder or something. What?"

Then he saw the look on my face. It was the Jenny's-morning-wreck-phone-call look.

I shoved the laptop toward him.

"Read it," I said. "Why would it even say that?"

"I'm not reading that," Jake said, pushing the laptop away.

"Read it," I said.

"I'm not reading it. What? Just tell me."

I started crying.

"It says Paul and Helen," I said.

The headline read YOUNG FAMILY GUNNED DOWN, and, though it can't be, it seemed to be about Paul and Helen. The article said Paul and Helen had been shot by an intruder and Helen was dead.

"No," Jake said.

I turned on my cell phone to call Courtney and David and saw I already had a message. Courtney wanted us to come Uptown, to where they had the baby and Rosie the pig to help while Paul was in the hospital. Helen and family had not been staying in their flooded house near us. When they had returned, they moved to a temporary apartment near a sublet lead Helen had sent me on St. Claude the year before. I wondered who had driven Rosie Uptown. Helen had come back to live and help because New Orleans felt like home to her. Why was New Orleans so shitty?

"I don't think I can handle this," Jake said.

When we got to Helen's friends' house, people were watching the yellow tape news on TV hoping it would explain something. Rosie was lazing around in a back room. Poor Rosie. We arranged a blanket on the floor for her nap.

"Does she eat apples?" someone, I think it was a painter, asked.

"I think Rosie likes cookies," I said.

I remembered brainstorming with Helen about a cheap and sturdy ramp plan a few years back because Rosie had gotten so hefty.

"She likes cat food," Jake said.

"She probably would like an apple," I said.

The next day, a bunch of sad people were standing in a hotel hallway. I was trying to make words come out to someone in Helen's family, when I caught a glimpse of the baby. The golden-haired toddler turned one tumbleset and then another down the dim hotel hall. He had been snacking. He was like a ray of light with jelly on his hands, a bright piece of Helen, a thin beam of light sparking down the dingy hotel hallway in this horrid place. Amazing.

A collective howl for all the New Orleans people killed over the years went up and pointed itself at everyone. There were generations of lost people the police and DA and politicians and citizens were too ineffectual to do anything about. Some people around town said, "Y'all don't care if a black person dies, only if a white person who went to college does. *How do you like it now?*" I didn't like it then, and I certainly didn't like it now. That black and white people both said things like that was a symptom of just how sad and sick New Orleans had gotten.

Jake and I had to film and interview people at the largest protest in New Orleans in decades. It was sickening and the worst front porch confessional yet.

After talking to dozens of people who had lost their family members to murder in New Orleans, after listening to tale after tale of our police and court system rarely holding anyone accountable for these crimes, the scope of the dysfunction became horribly clear. I met the Danziger Bridge families and countless others. Counting up dreadful and cheesy murder memorial T-shirts on fellow New Orleanians, including the new one I was wearing with sweet Helen smiling eerily on my chest, the toll of decades of unceasing street violence was dreadfully clear.

In the midst of all this, Jake got the dumb gun out of the guest room and put it back under the bed. Abandoned houses were on all sides of us. Our fence was still down. After what happened to Helen and Paul, I was scared to take the dogs out at night to pee in the backyard. A lot of us were afraid. Banana Republic afraid.

For some reason I thought of this glib Nola T-shirt, LOUISIANA—THIRD WORLD AND PROUD OF IT. I hoped I never saw anyone wearing it again.

After a few more shootings in our neighborhood, we freaked and drove to Mississippi for a night to take refuge at Brad and Sam's. On the way there, Jake said, "I refuse to take a bullet for this town."

When we returned, I locked the door and sent an e-mail to our neighborhood association. During all the treated lumber versus untreated lumber and reduced footprint of New Orleans debates, some neighbors had occasionally helped give perspective. Sometimes when you were really lost, when a contractor was dumping someone else's asbestos on your sidewalk, sometimes some neighbor blocks away knew what to do.

From: Cherylwagner
Subject: Mid-City Slum!

Mid-City is turning into a giant slum filled with junkies, knife fighting roofers, and people who have taken to shooting at people who they see climbing on their roof (Banks Street . . . near Mona's, at the "boarding house" btwn S. Scott and Cortez a few nights ago). Squatters are murdering each other on the 400 block of S. Genois (yesterday) and people feel plenty free to light up the occasional crack pipe on the street in the middle of the day (S. Clark Street, near Cleveland, about three days ago and I'm sure a lot more often than that). Life between Tulane, Jeff Davis, Carrollton, and Canal is looking worse than it did 6 months ago if that is at all possible (and sadly it seems that it is). Has the city unofficially/officially decided to let this area become a slum?

A nearby neighbor wrote back. It was Mr. Joe, our friend down the street working hard to restore his house from his FEMA trailer. He owned the miracle house where the roofer had fallen and bounced and lived. Many days we had complained together outside and laughed.

From: Joe S.
Subject: re: Mid-City Slum!

No. I live here and I have great neighbors both home owners and renters. However, we do need to keep vigilant and keep working to protect the quality of life. We are an economic, socially, racially mixed neighborhood. Our residents are of all classes, a true melting pot. There are negatives that cause concern as you have indicated but there are many more positives. We need to keep fighting to protect our neighbor.

Joe

My neighbor made a lot of sense. I just didn't know if I could afford to believe him again.

For our second Mardi Gras season since the flood, I baked some brownies and iced them with a hot pink, grinning skeleton for Chris's annual Skeleton Krewe party. I thought my stolen pit bull Jesus might be there. It wasn't.

I was surprised how many papier-mâché skulls he and his marching club members had made and amassed over the past few years for their absurdist death parades. Oversized human, pelican, and robot skulls took up so many nooks and crannies of his house, one room was beginning to resemble the catacombs. Their annual grotesque homage to the old New Orleans Mardi Gras day Bone gangs seemed particularly apt this year.

Watching NOPD point blame from their FEMA trailers and bicker with the district attorney while his staff fell apart inside a defunct nightclub was disheartening. Seeing a local city councilman use Helen's bright front porch in our neighborhood as a bully pulpit was disgusting. My tolerance for the surreal ended.

Losing Helen sapped us of what was left. Jake and I decided we needed to get serious again about our New Orleans exit plan.

We had vowed to get our Plan B (and C and D) in place before last hurricane season, and we hadn't. So far we had failed to produce any plan that we liked as much as New Orleans. But Anytown, Anywhere was gaining quick.

Since Clo was too old and sickly to walk that far, we took Buster to Helen's jazz funeral. He waddled along next to one of the brass bands for blocks, but by the time the procession was down by the deserted and shuttered Lafitte projects, Buster gave out. At first I had an idea that we could each take one side of Buster, like we had done with Helen's backyard glider. That didn't last long. Soon Jake and I had to take turns carrying him. When I couldn't carry him at all, Jake slung Buster like a sack of potatoes over his shoulder and he panted at the the tuba player the rest of the way.

"Why in the world did we bring this dog?" Jake said, breaking a sweat.

"Because Clo can't make it. Because he's Rosie's friend," I said. "Kids like him."

"Buster can't make it, either. And he was scared of Rosie," Jake said.

"Not of her. Of all the snorting. He still liked going over there."

Instead of feeling cheered by the celebration of Helen's life, by a few of her friends dressed like jumbo chickens handing out cupcakes to cars and little kids at stoplights, by the dancing under the interstate, by the brass brand playing "I'll Fly Away," the whole cutting loose of our friend left me depressed. It felt like a funeral not only for Helen, but for our dream that New Orleans could be whole for everyone again.

In the weeks that followed, Jake sprouted a short fuse. He became Disaster Jake Plus, then Disaster Jake X-Treme, then Rowdy

Roddy Disaster Jake. He grumped and cussed and revved his paint-spattered truck. When he tried to work on the house, he slammed lumber around. Clo didn't notice, but it made Buster hide in the other room.

I wasn't much better. At the stoplight in our neighborhood on the utter skid row of Tulane Avenue where the transient men who followed disaster workers hung with the prostitutes and dealers, I saw a man with a four-foot mullet dressed like a low-budget assassin from a nunchuk movie and thought, God save me from a death with a punchline. There was of course no good way to go, especially soon, but I specifically did not want to be taken out by any of the flood characters in my neighborhood—not by the methed-out mullet man, not by the guy who pretended to be both mentally retarded and a veteran in a wheelchair, and especially not by Disaster Elf, the guy in the tights on the bicycle who wore the winter hat all year long.

I did not feel like being outside in my garden anymore. I pictured something dreadful and armed lurking in all the surrounding abandoned houses. Jake and I stopped working on the inside and started working on the backyard fence. I had to be able to take the dogs out by myself at night again.

Jake and his old guitarist had pulled down the shed with ropes and ran as it crashed, and we had all carted it to the curb piece by piece. A big cracked concrete slab with plumbing marked where it used to stand. We dug holes and poured concrete for fence posts. We checked out Dave and Marcelle's crazy ten-foot fence and drew up plans for our seven-foot one that I wished could be twelve.

Pastor Jim noticed the hubbub and came over. Late one night he had helped hold a ladder while I climbed up to a second-story ledge and into our bedroom window. We had locked and shuttered ourselves out. He thought I shouldn't be climbing ladders at night, and before this all started I would have agreed. But I would rather brave the ladder than break another thing I would have to fix. I think he felt he should keep an eye on us.

"That's a big fence," he said. "Who you keeping out?"

"You," I joked.

All our posts were set and we built most of the frame. Our backyard was big by New Orleans standards—and long. My arms burned from holding up two-by-fours while Jake drilled.

"It's not that big," Jake said. "We're going seven. She wanted to go eight."

"I wanted to go ten," I said. "We compromised."

"That might be against code," Pastor Jim remarked.

"We're blocking some of your back bedroom light, but we're leaving the alley free," I reminded him, in case he was complaining. "Also now we can't peep in on you."

"I'm not worried as long as we can both still use that alley," he said. "I'm just saying the city could always come back at you later."

"Then we'd tear it down," Jake said.

"That lady down the street built a two-story house in her backyard," I said. "The city isn't doing anything. Who's going to stop us? It's hog-wild around here."

"That's true," Pastor Jim said.

"Yeah, we'll take the risk," Jake said.

yellow flowers, yellow letter

I wanted the tub out of the upstairs hallway and back in its bathroom. We had one other tub that worked, but I was sick of tripping over this one. I was telling Mom about it on the phone.

"Y'all don't need to be doing all that," Mom suddenly announced. "Leave some of that alone."

She was growing impatient with how much time and energy we poured into fixing the house. It was as if she, along with every other unflooded person, forgot how this mess started to begin with.

"Then who's going to do it?" I said.

"Nobody," she said.

"If we take a break," I said, "I'm scared we may never restart."

"That's just why you need to take a break and leave the other half for a while," she said.

"We may not have a choice," I said. "I'm exhausted."

I had been thinking a lot about our quality of life and prolonged lack thereof. Everyone did not get to live to be eighty. I didn't want my life to swirl down the dirty drain of mind-numbing work; it was exactly what I had *never* wanted. I had seen this new life coming when the flood started but did not know exactly what shape it would take.

For a while, when I had some kind of end in sight, I felt like a temporary construction worker. But then one day when I was in the front yard with Sheetrock mud smeared on my arms, hosing off my taping knife, a man stopped his truck and tried to hire me. It was the three-hundred-pound Hispanic foreman who had converted a few regular New Orleans houses in our neighborhood to boarding houses. When Jake's old guitarist and I were building another picket fence, the foreman had stopped to sketch our design. Soon after on Banks Street around the corner and behind my fence, I saw him playing cards on his front porch, sitting under some international long distance card posters.

Seeing me cleaning my tools, he stopped his truck.

"Now you Sheetrock?" he asked. "You want a job with me?"

"I don't really know how to do this," I said. "You don't want me."

"You doing it?" he said.

"Yeah, but only a little. Only here," I said. "I'm retiring and quitting after."

"Then come see me for job," he said, waving and driving off.

With no end in sight now, I decided to grab more time for projects I had formerly been interested in, before I totally transformed into what others like the foreman saw in me. But between construction work, paid work, and total flood aggravation, I had little time left over. I had committed to helping a friend with a writing project, but with all the generators and table saws and concrete jackhammers of the Sewerage and Water Board on my street, often I had to wear earplugs or flee Uptown.

We were still the lucky ones. And we were burned out. We knew people going into tons of debt to fix their houses even though the levees and canal walls weren't properly repaired. Sometimes these homeowners hired contractors who would cash their checks and never do the work. No one had any way to stop them. So far our half-DIY plan had us back in the house with mostly floated but unpainted walls and a working bathroom and kitchen. We had been robbed of only a few thousand dollars. Still we were far from finishing. Either we were in over our heads, the house was too big, or both.

The day the yellow letter came we were enjoying a rare balmy, blue-sky sensation. We were grimy and saw-dusted, yes, but we were happy. For a few weeks it had warmed up. Not shivering whenever I was in the house had brightened my mood considerably.

The yellow cassia tree I had replanted the previous year was huge and sunny and blooming early. The irises I had planted in the neighbor's Mary grotto across the street were tall and green. Wild onions had joined them in the patch. Jake and I had put the finishing touches on the backyard fence, and we were sitting on the front porch, with the dogs sniffing the breeze.

No longer did we drive across town to pick up our mail at the flooded neighborhood mail sorting center; it came to our own mailbox. And today the mailman handed us the Road Home envelope we had been awaiting for months.

Jake had been dreading the yellow letter. Over the holidays, a Road Home worker had scheduled our assessment. She was an Asian immigrant wearing an Axl Rose bandana and we had had difficulty communicating. She had driven over from Texas and bragged about her high case turnover rate. "If they want to see me bad enough, they'll meet me," she'd said. "They won't care what day." She waved her hands at Jake and cried, "Shut up! Shut up!" when he tried to give her details from our insurance company.

"Uh oh," Jake now said, opening the envelope slowly.

I read over his shoulder.

The Road Home offers assistance to homeowners . . .
Please refer to the information about the calculations for more information about why your compensation grant was zero.

"What does that mean?" I said. "It's nothing?"

"Hush," Jake said.

I scanned the Factors Used to Calculate Benefits Estimates. The Estimated Pre-Storm Value was incorrect. And the Estimated Damage to Your Home was incorrect. Our insurance company had declared our home a total loss even though it was theoretically fixable. This was based on the amount it would cost to fix our house if we did not conduct an Amish barn raising.

"I see the word zero but I don't see the number," I said.

"Hush," Jake said.

"What the hell?" I said. "Why did those people we met with less water, no wind, and more insurance money get so much then?"

"I'm trying to read it!"

One way I had been coping with the roller coaster was by declaring temporary residency in the land of diminished expectations. For months I had been saying that we were not going to get any help from Road Home just as we had gotten no trailer. And, oh well, whatever. But since then a number of people we knew with less damage had been promised sixty, seventy, eighty thousand in assistance. I had dared to dream that maybe I would not spend all my spare time for another year sanding and refinishing floors and painting. Or that at least the determination would be transparent and fair. That had been stupid. My friend's mom had just a slab left in St. Bernard and had gotten nothing. Like almost all of the flood bureaucracy thus far, the determinations process seemed dysfunctional and utterly random.

"Forget about the zero for a minute," Jake said. "Look here. Why does it say we have less rooms than we do? Does it say we have carpet and sliding glass doors? We don't."

I read a few more lines on the house assessment form. "Oh. It's not our house," I said. "That's someone else's house with our address on it."

Jake shook his head. He pointed to another page. "It is our

house. There's our sliding pocket doors. It's just our house *and* someone else's house. It's two different houses put together on the same form."

The yellow letter signaled the start of another gruesome, protracted bureaucratic battle. No way would we accept a determination made on a form that had so much basic information wrong. Still we were lucky. We did not need the permission of the yellow letter writers to reclaim our home. But we knew many who did. Their houses rotted around us.

I hoped these flood years had been among the worst of my entire life and, having them under my belt, I could cross them off the list and go on. Yet I also didn't know if I believed in a set allotment of only a few major aggravations or catastrophes anymore. If I brought things like that up to Jake, he sometimes said scary, why-brush-your-teeth-at-all type things like "That's what adulthood is. One tragedy to the next."

Jake had turned thirty about seven months after the flood mess began. Since then he had sprouted a few gray hairs. Sometimes I heard him talking like a grizzled, old man, telling people that the flood had sheared a decade off his life. And now, after what had happened to his stepsister and Helen, Jake was nurturing a few new rotgut beliefs. One was that when elderly people said things like "life is good" what they really meant was not that life was good, per se, but that nothing devastating had befallen them in the prior six months. It was disaster vision and it wasn't true.

I wanted to challenge Jake on this before it took deeper root. When his next birthday rolled around, what a relief to see him crowd onto the glider next to friends, drinking strawberry beer and eating crawfish and Doberge cake. He and a friend schemed how to construct a $4,000 video camera lens from junk parts. A late-night Toobin' tournament commenced, and many greener comrades went down.

For some reason I didn't fully understand or even necessarily agree with (like being tired, or how big and beautiful the re-planted angel trumpet flower trees were now getting, or because the I-Have-Oranges-and-Bananas-Man was back cruising our street in his fruit truck singing his song and had said, "We do good in the French Quarter. Around here, it's dead . . . but we still come"), by the end of April, instead of being 90 percent sure we needed to leave New Orleans, we were back to being 55 percent sure we might be trying to stay.

Chapter 21

adieu

When Jake found the twin lumps one night while taking Clo's cape off and stroking her neck, he was worried. But I thought Clotilde Robichaux was rough and tumble. The vet had been calling her senior for a while. On the dog levee I had met people with magic bassets who pushed it to sixteen or eighteen. She always seemed like those bassets. Clo had a lot to live for—eating, sleeping, ruling Buster with an increasingly iron paw, and gulping the breeze from the back of a pickup. She had just dug herself a cool bed under the Lakeview jasmine tree in the backyard. When she wasn't digging holes next to me, she chewed sticks under the jasmine while I gardened.

Yes, Clo had swallowed some slate, suffered a number of kidney problems, and since she had lost her hearing, staked out more and more territory. And sometimes she snapped at Buster, giving him an evil, clouded eye. I felt rotten about the roofing slate removal procedure and, though she was almost fourteen, worried that her kidney problems were my fault from having her live in a construction site in a possibly toxic flood zone. But even though she was frequently sleepy and we had to carry her up and down our steep stairs, she still enjoyed treeing City Park squirrels and eating Popeyes chicken.

Tanio flew to town again. He did not get out his soldering

tools or touch his arcade cabinets, but instead threw himself onto our new couch.

"I don't know if I want to come back here anymore. Ever. I'm serious. You, my dad, now poor Clo. Jesus! This place is an emotional sinkhole," he said. "I can't take it."

I knew what he meant, but I didn't know what to say. Life wasn't all theremins and trips to San Jose to see lightning shoot from gigantic Tesla coils. I wish it was.

"You said you needed to be here," I said. "I don't want to be here, either. I can't stand it."

Clo had put up with so much doctoring in her life that she now panicked whenever she went to the vet. After we had received her grim test results, I didn't see any reason to make her go back. So the vet was coming to the house.

Pastor Jim, the math teacher, and other neighbors kept knocking on our front porch window. When we needed a ladder or a wheelbarrow or a spare piece of wood, we bugged them just as much. Seeing Jake and I standing around with our chins on the ground, they wanted to know what was going on. I had long ago noticed the flood took our privacy. But I usually didn't need it.

One weird thing that only disaster people understand is the complete and tiresome way a disaster insinuates itself into everything. Like a black-and-white movie suddenly Technicolor terrible, everything is tinted by the disaster. People who do not live, eat, and breathe a disaster for years have no reference point for this. Sometimes they think a man is exaggerating when he says, "The flood took my mama" if that particular mother did not specifically drown in the flood. But all the people touched by disaster just nod their heads yes. They know that elderly mother died from grief or stress or living her twilight years in shock and mess or maybe lived and just wasn't the same ever again. They know *the flood took* is not just a figure of speech. The same water took someone else's marriage or lover, job, or spirit. The flood took my dog.

Clotilde Robichaux was no more. When I got her from an old man in Terrytown on the West Bank of the Mississippi River, he lifted her from her blanket in a playpen. She was hand sized with droopy ears and preposterously cute. He set her on the ground and grabbed his fishing pole. He cast her a weighted pink feather and she swatted it with fat paws. When I said I wanted her, he said, "Aw, now you're taking my heart."

Because we are home, because we are still in New Orleans, we are able to walk down the street to the bayou to hear a brass band play songs about happiness following grief. Maybe it's the sky mirrored in the bayou or the company of friends, but the music I couldn't really hear at Helen's second line I could almost hear that day.

Chapter 22

the happy dutch

Friends who wanted to help save New Orleans also decided it was their duty to save me from it. A Russian friend who spent his childhood in New Orleans, whom I had known since I was fifteen, scared me during dinner one night. He said, "Cheryl, I have friends from South Africa. They had *everything*. The fear, they couldn't live with it. One day they just had to leave." I wasn't sure exactly what he meant by the analogy.

In the past, sometimes people would give me the Leave New Orleans speech, but it was usually a career talk, and not everyone at the same time. Sometimes, it seemed the new Leave New Orleans speech might be the same old talk about maximizing my earning potential back with a vengeance. Other times, it seemed different. People could not detect the snail's progress we saw. Maybe they just did not believe what I hoped—that mess and crime could not go on forever because too many people were too sick of it. I hoped I was right.

Pete used to sometimes live on my couch and had since emigrated to the Netherlands. He had been trying to get me to check out Amsterdam for years. Our bumbling police department and mayor were predicting a summer "uptick" in murder because things always get worse in New Orleans when the temperature soars. Because the federal government chose to take a hands-off approach to the bedlam they helped create, Jake and I decided to get out of Dodge for a bit. We planned to go house-sit for Pete and take our long-overdue New Orleans break.

A cinematographer friend was living in his friend's puppet studio. He wanted to move into the finished part of our house while we were gone.

"Daryn *wants* to stay here?" I asked Jake time and again.

"That's what he says," Jake said.

"He knows the neighbors are going to ask him for tools and to help lift heavy stuff and that there's jackhammering and buzz-sawing a lot?" I said. "He knows we only have a little air-conditioning?"

"I told him," Jake said. "It's better than it was. By a ton."

"Yeah. But everybody who doesn't live over here says how can we stand it. Two years of hearing that makes you feel like you're crazy," I said. "So Daryn thinks this isn't a terrible neighborhood . . . interesting. He knows about the shed thief and the guy kicking doors in and the copper guys and that we have one next-door neighbor and the rest abandoned around us?"

"I told him," Jake said. "We have less mugging. This is Uptown to him."

Apparently since Daryn had taken to walking St. Claude Avenue at night with a baseball bat, he was game. He preferred flood thieves to muggers. And he would water my plants.

Hurricane season was due to churn up again while we were out of town. We had taken down our French louvered shutters. We tried to make sure we had solid shutters that closed tight for every window this second storm season. But, once again, our best just wasn't good enough.

After helping the carpenter build the kitchen cabinets, I had helped sand, putty, prime, and paint more than thirty shutters. But then I switched tasks like I wasn't supposed to, so some of the shutters remained only primed. We were still a few shutters short of maximum wind protection, but we were close. This made me feel like a loser, but a slightly different type of loser than I was pre-flood.

Right before we left, Pastor Jim pulled a gun over our shared fence on the new shed thief that replaced the old shed thief. He had held him there while he called the cops, but then the shed thief ran. We were driving to get some stuff for our trip when Jake's cell phone rang. It was Pastor Jim, winded and running. He said come to the corner of S. Telemachus quick. He was chasing the shed thief up Palmyra until the cops showed up.

"I don't want to chase the shed thief!" I said. "For God's sake, don't go chase the shed thief! It's not worth it. That's not our job."

"No shit. I'm not chasing any shed thief," Jake said, swinging the truck back around toward our neighborhood.

"Why are you turning around then?"

"I feel bad leaving him hanging like that."

"Why didn't he just call the police?" I said. "He's going to give himself a heart attack."

"You know why. Here, call the police and tell them where they're running. Tell them it's a white guy with dark hair in a blue sweatshirt."

"Huh," I said. "You think it's Black Van?"

Since our confrontation over the little boy, the drug addict that fenced stuff on the corner had turned up squatting various displaced people's houses on streets near us. But after he got put out of the last one, we hadn't seen him for a while.

"Just call," Jake said. "I'm going by Pastor Jim's. They're already long gone from there."

A young New Orleans guy with a wife and small son had bought the dollhouse looming over us. We were rooting for them to shut that back wall and live in that house. If they did, we would be down to only one other dollhouse on our block. No one wanted Black Van or some other shed thief to get all his tools.

Out of the country, Jake and I discovered we got along better without the grating symphony of generators and jackhammers and buzz saws always ripping on our street. We felt strangely relaxed when no one was pointing a gun at anyone or mentioning someone who did. When Dutch or British people asked, we said we're from New Orleans. Though it was nearly two years after the televised humiliation, I was surprised that people still got that stricken, funeral look on their face. I wondered if I ever would say I'm from New Orleans again and see the old look that used to come over people's faces. That mild disapproval or sly grin. I missed getting irritated when strangers said, "You must really party a *lot*."

A cab driver had interesting observations on our shared flood control issues and lectured us kindly on global warming, but other Dutchies began to get on my nerves. While we were staying in North Amsterdam taking the ferry into town every day, I started a catalog of Dutch misbehaviors. Fistfighting on the ferry. Making a rottweiler jog while wearing sunglasses every day, not just for special occasions. Haircuts like north Louisiana 1985. Rocking to old disco on the town square. Projecting a purportedly laid-back, actually uptight "social order at all costs!" smoke *here*/prostitute *there*/bike-only-where-and-when-told attitude. Many Dutch people were gruff and grumpy, even though they all had health care and no one was shooting guns in the air in anger or for special occasions like New Year's and the Fourth of July.

Jake biked and biked all day and into the evening. He decided I was wound too tight. One day, I freaked out because not only could I not get an iced coffee, but I couldn't get any coffee in a paper or go-cup at all anywhere, and I had brought some editing work. I was stranded and coffeeless in North Amsterdam.

"In New Orleans, someone would at least make you an iced coffee in an MRE bag," I said. "What is this crap?"

"This is why you can't leave New Orleans," Jake said pointedly. "You think everyone needs to walk around with a cup in their hand."

Tucked in my friend's safe little apartment above a safe little Dutch bike shop, cradled in the arms of my strong Dutch levees, I had the worst dreams. In one, Clo was alive and crying. Green monster tears oozed down her basset cheeks. In another, some guy down my street in New Orleans shot someone and then went up and down the block threatening people to keep quiet. When he got to me, I said honestly, "I'm not worried, I have no clue what went on down there." "You better be," he said, mouth choked with dull gold teeth. "Your daddy *bought* that gun."

Jake was in the bedroom shutting the curtain and piling pillows on top of the little windows. It stayed light really late. We woke up hungry every morning from the smell of bread rising from the ovens of the bakery next door. I told him about my dreams.

"Sick," Jake said. "Can you not tell me that? I had some dreams the other night, too, and decided to spare you."

"What about?" I said.

"I'm not saying," he said. "I don't want to bring it back. I'm going to that film-thing tomorrow. It's nice to be able to bike at night. I feel like if somebody here wanted to mug you, they wouldn't also kill you."

I was worried that prolonged exposure to the New Orleans mayhem might change us into two small, suspicious and fearful people we had not originally been. I did not want to become a pair of whacked, pseudo-sentries who saw snipers on corners where before we had seen only children. That seemed like a miserable person to be.

On the phone recently, my neuroscientist-Sheetrocker friend Jeff said he was afraid for his elderly parents on Jackson Avenue. I told him I didn't like going over to their neighborhood since he had told us about the drunk Mexican guy breaking into their house and walking around in his mom's dress. Plus we had seen some teens sucker-punch a guy off a bicycle near there, too. Deep in his post-Sheetrock doc in neurobiowhatever at Harvard, Jeff cautioned that I might be altering my neurological pathways just like his old lab rats by exposing myself to constant fear and stress. Everyone had said New Orleans after the storm might be toxic. Maybe the dreams were proof. I asked Jeff if he had done his experiments in reverse, but he had not.

I decided that the Dutch reported higher degrees of contentment not because it was so awesomely perfect there but simply because they slept better in their beds at night. Their government's commitment to modern flood control allowed them to doze without one hand clutching an inflatable pirogue. Their social programs seemed to create less deprived children walking around with guns in their sleeves and waistbands.

Pete's little boy in Amsterdam was the same age and blond like Helen's toddler. He wanted me to put on a helmet. He scooted me around the apartment on the tiny backseat of his baby bike. Seeing him giggle and bounce around his mother made me sad.

One afternoon while Jake was in town and I was sitting at the table working, I heard a Dutch brass band strike up outside in the neighborhood square. It was a festival. The band tooted the same tuba and trumpets, but they sounded exactly the opposite of what a New Orleans brass band might sound like. Soon Dutch disco singers shimmied and spun near some garbage cans on a small stage. Then, out of the blue, the familiar strains of a Louis Armstrong tune floated up through my window.

"No way," I said.

I hung off the balcony to get a better look. Jake was going to be sorry he missed it. An old Dutch Satchmo impersonator, one hand raised, began to croak "What a Wonderful World." He sang so deep that his face turned red as a sausage. He sang like he might hurt himself. He had decided New Orleans and jazz required this almost death metal deep, gravelly voice. He sweated and gave it all he had, moaning and pulling this voice from the soles of his feet.

Mom surprised us by getting a ticket to Europe. Turned out for years she had been stockpiling frequent flier miles buying groceries. Since our relationship had degenerated into a lot of worry and vacuuming and painting, I looked forward to seeing Budapest with Mom.

In Hungary, Mom wanted to try out her settlement Hungarian. She wanted to see what real Hungarians looked like these days instead of the Louisiana Hungarians we had both grown accustomed to. On a hot pink plane on the way there, she nudged me and smiled. Grandpa was gone, but there on the plane was one of those short Hungarian men who looked Asian like her father. He was such the spitting image of Grandpa that it was kind of scary.

In Budapest, I was thinking about how Mom's people were economic refugees. I was wondering if they had to leave, just decided to go on their own, or if their friends first gave them a lot of Leave Hungary talks. But Mom was not thinking about that kind of thing. She was busy eating these dumplings she had not had since her mother died. She heard people sing songs her grandfather sang to her in the fields when she was a girl.

birth of a buzzkill

Courtney made these waterline markers on happy colored tin and hung them around town on telephone poles. They commemorated the depth levels for various floods. There was Bonnet Carré Crevasse—1871, Grand Isle Hurricane—1909, May Rainstorm—1995, Hurricane Katrina—2005, and so on. She brought me an electric blue 2005 flood marker to hang in my house. We were in my living room—one of my two normal, painted, and floors finished zones.

"Yeah, but look here," I said, showing her a scummy ring in my front window. "My real waterline. I've washed that a million times and it still won't come off. It's some kind of crazy water in that one spot. I probably need to change out the glass pane."

"So you don't like my marker," she said.

"No, I kind of like it. But I'll like it more in a few months when that's off the window. Thanks. I'll put it up then."

Performance artists decided to set up spectacles in people's flooded neighborhoods. Later in the summer, when we had gotten back from our trip, Courtney and I went to watch an artist box himself. Returning to New Orleans, I had promised myself not to get sucked back into the flood-zone vortex. I was making an effort to get out of flood-world and spend time doing anything I used to do before I always had a tool in my hand.

But Jake didn't feel like it. He said, "If you want to stand out in

Hollygrove and watch some douche box himself all night, that's on you." Once I brought Jake to an experimental theater and some performance poet dragged him onstage to slow-dance. He had never really forgiven me.

On the edge of another flooded neighborhood near a FEMA trailer, the shirtless artist in shorts and boxing gloves had set up an outdoor boxing ring to box himself until sunrise. Courtney and I stood ringside with a few of the guy's friends. I predicted a flood-stressed individual might take him up on his invitation and jump into the ring, and he would get his ass kicked. After a while, an old neighborhood man in a hat wandered over and hung on the ropes and wanted to shoot the bull with him, but the boxer was curt and serious. If it was supposed to be a metaphor for flood-life or something, he was way off. The boxer would need that man in the hat in the middle of the night sometime. He should step out of the ring and help that neighbor carry something. He should say something funny so the man would keep an eye out for him when the real flood weirdos arrived.

By September, Courtney and I were standing at Kinko's on St. Charles photocopying our friends' faces. We had been out putting up Crimestoppers flyers where the police suggested in the neighborhood near where Helen was killed. The boundaries were so large that we had run out. I had tacked up more than my share of friends' band flyers in the past, and Courtney had posted art stuff. Our friends' faces smiling from a Crimestoppers flyer was a dismal turn of events.

Seeing the happy couple grinning on the flyers made strangers upset. A man in a rusty truck wearing a gold crucifix had grabbed my hands. He said God was blessing me, but I did not feel like I had helped anything.

Courtney's husband David drove. Courtney and I would hop out in front of a convenience store, staple a few up, walk to the next pole past some kids and drunk guys, and staple a few more. The longer we spent stapling flyers to telephone poles in the Ninth Ward, the madder I got.

I hated that the police thought that someone in this neighborhood knew who did this. I hated that they couldn't find the killer. I felt like they weren't really looking. I couldn't stand the thought of that ruinous guy running his mouth on his front stoop watching us staple flyers.

I got back in the car and slammed the door. "If I told you a year ago we'd be doing this would you believe me?" I said.

"No," David said. "I wouldn't want to."

"I'm helping but I'm dubious," I said.

"That's a very big surprise," David joked.

"What are these supposed to do? Make someone who knows who did it remember and feel guilty and tell? If they felt so guilty, they would've told in the first place."

"Supposedly Crimestoppers gets tips from the reward all the time. I don't know if they feel guilty. Maybe they need the money," David said.

"Putting these up makes me feel like a vigilante. And worse than that—a vigilante who's doing a bad job," I said. "A lame-ass vigilante. Sucks."

A few weeks later, Courtney projected a video piece at a gallery in town. A Japanese magnolia lost its pale pink petals as a hard shadow shot by. The shot missed and flipped the bruised petal and it came floating safely down. It was a wish.

Around Halloween, Jake and I stepped into our backyard and almost got knocked over by the sound of really loud, really fake reggae. I stood on a broken bench and peered over our rebuilt fence. Past the other abandoned dollhouse about to collapse on the corner that everyone said rats would stream out of like a horror movie once the city finally tore it down, there it was. The world's worst oasis. Twinkle-lit against the disaster zone by globe yard lights—a bunch of thirty-somethings getting irie.

I pictured the lady on that block turning up her tiny TV, the aluminum of her FEMA trailer tinny buzzing that lame rock-steady. I thought of Mr. Slim on my block in his trailer in his sister's driveway with his windows cracked just enough so the formaldehyde would not get him but the Rastafari would. I thought of the fire that had recently torn through the upstairs of that sister's house right after they had just finished repairing it.

I thought of myself. Over two years of running generators and drills and saws and sanders and vacs and listening to others do the same had changed me. Since we'd had to live in our messed-up house in our messed-up neighborhood for so long, my ears were tired. And tired of hearing me say they were tired.

Around the flood zone, mine was an old, common, and boring story told by a bunch of suddenly old, common, and boring people. I never really thought much before about how a person became a Drag—I just avoided them. But now I knew. My flooded New Orleans neighborhood was one big Drag factory. I was hot off the assembly line.

I dreaded unflooded friends asking me how "things" were going. They didn't want to ask and I didn't want to answer. They were curious, but people on the other side of town had long since moved on. I did not enjoy subjecting people to boring tirades or insta-rages, and I knew I might. When someone wouldn't drop it, I tried to answer quick.

"They sent this lady in an Axl Rose bandana and she wrote down we have vinyl siding and we don't," I said. This was shorthand for eight months duking it out with the Road Home Program, Louisiana's surreal answer to housing recovery.

Sometimes the neighborhood seemed to be getting safer, but

then something odd would happen. A stranger had mysteriously been shot in the butt while walking a few blocks away. But we broke our rule about walking the gauntlet at night and went to investigate the reggae anyway.

Weedy and uninhabited for over two years, the two-story wood house a block away had suddenly kick-started and revved to life. Light radiated from all the ten-foot windows. Out front, a stubby catering trailer that looked like a baby FEMA trailer sat across the street from the real thing.

In recent months, I'd noticed some expensive looking contractors busting ass at that house. And by expensive I mean contractors with tools. Men not scraped off the corner of Tulane and Carrollton after scoring their morning meth. The kind who used a Portalet instead of someone's yard, did not steal your plumbing or squat your house and burn it down with their hobo Sterno in the pitch of night. The kind that if the Road Home Program ever unmixed up our file we might get for a month so we didn't have to either give up or finish fixing everything ourselves. Ever since we had gone on hiatus to get back to our normal selves and work before we lost both, our production had ground to a weekends-and-nights-only-type crawl.

We were lucky. FEMA had bumped us from the trailer list twice, so we did not get gassed with formaldehyde. We were alive. We still had health and time and each other and employment to brace us. Still we were over two years slogging to the finish line, and the finish line kept receding. *Losers!* I was starting to hear the bystanders shout.

Because I no longer went to Mass or said the rosaries Mom still pressed on me, Jake and I had added feeble attempts at zenning out to our nervous breakdown avoidance regimen. This devolved into Jake sneaking up on me and barking, "Unwrinkle your forehead!"

It made me jump. "Unwrinkle *your* forehead!" I sometimes snapped back.

"I can't." He shrugged.

Sometimes Jake pressed his finger between my eyebrows like there was a RESET button.

The reggae thumped from the house's backyard. As we walked up, we saw Chris lurking out front near a catering trailer. Even though it wasn't Halloween proper, he was wearing his Skeleton Krewe jumpsuit painted with chalky bones. Jake nudged me.

"Busted!" I yelled, rattling him.

Chris grinned and shook his head. "Hey, I thought about walking down and knocking on y'all's door," he said.

"Call from our porch," Jake said. "Doorbell's still out."

"You need to fix that shit," Chris said. He thumbed toward the house. "Y'all know them?"

"Not really, they're kind of new," I said. "We just came to see who on their first night back in years is rocking people in their trailers with some crap reggae."

Chris gave me a funny look.

"A lot of people still work all week and get up early to fix their houses on the weekends," I school-marmed, surprising myself. "It's kind of rude."

One good thing about living in New Orleans used to be that in most neighborhoods there weren't many of the kind of people who acted like the kind of pain in the ass I was being. Hearing myself speak up for people's right not to be rocked in their trailers, I heard myself sounding just like some maw maw. I did not like it. *If the music's too loud, DAD, you're too old!*

"Aw, come on. It's his contractor's band," Chris said. "He told them if they finished quick they could play his backyard."

Jake laughed and shook his head.

"Aw, lighten up. Come watch one song," Chris said, giving me a look.

It was the recovery buzzkill look. I got it a lot lately. I was a recovery buzzkill when I said that the new Neighborhood Association posters were hippie-cheesy because they featured a black woman on a porch strumming a guitar for double-dutching white kids, which I had never noticed going on in New Orleans much less Mid-City. I was a recovery buzzkill when I suggested to disaster carpetbaggers that no one wanted to buy a $200,000 condo next to a flophouse and that a one-bedroom shotgun was not a three-bedroom no matter which way they sliced it. When I asked the loopy cat-rescue lady to set buckets of Friskies on her own porch instead of making a rat haven out of some displaced person's house, that made me a recovery buzzkill, too. It was people like me who were holding back the recovery.

"At least have a po-boy," Chris said.

"Who has a po-boy catering truck?" Jake demanded, getting in on the buzzkill.

"And a spacewalk. It's in the back. Come on, they just finished their house!" he said, getting irritated. "You don't want to at least take the tour?"

I shook my head and stayed firmly on the sidewalk. "Nah," I said. "I have to live here. You don't know how it is over here now."

Whole new social rules were in play since the flood. For years before the flood, Jake's old band practiced in our living room and blasted our neighbors several times a week. Back then I would've sat on the porch with a go-cup in my hand swinging my feet to some neighbor kid's Lil' Boosie Bad Azz or just about anything. But not now. I didn't want my neighbors to come out of their trailers and half-finished houses with toilet paper stuffed in their ears and see me shaking my moneymaker to some contractor-Jah. I knew all of them. They were tired.

The I'm-finished-and-you're-not party had become a feature of the post-flood landscape. The first one we had been invited to was some months before in the JazzFest house—after our British musician friend sold it, after the contractor people from Georgia finished it, and before the hard-luck family squatted it. We had ventured down the street with extreme trepidation. We had lights by then, but others didn't. The post-flood renovators had flaunted their party house privilege and never realized it.

When people finished even the most ostentatious renovations they dumped boatloads of money few people had into, they expected people in the neighborhood to celebrate with them. We weren't finished, so we didn't have the party. I had been on a few flood renovation house tours featuring gleaming countertops and swirlpooly megatubs only to slink back home afterward to my own wreck. Sometimes I felt bad about what we had finished— our new gutters, picket fence, and green paint job, my fancy new electricity—and hoped it didn't make my trailer neighbors sad.

Judging from how Road Home was going, I knew that when we did finish, other people still wouldn't be. For months Jake had gone by their offices, talked to dozens of people dozens of times, saying, turn him down, fine. But before they made any final determination, he only wanted the information recorded on *his* form to be about *his* house at *his* address. It had become a quest to plant a bulwark for common sense.

Dealing with Road Home was the final circle of hell. When one of our neighbors went to one of his Road Home appointments, the representative had put her hand on his arm and said they should breathe and pray. It scared him when he realized he needed it. The changing rules and organizational structure spun people back and forth until they were twisted inside. It was like a very advanced form of military torture.

One day after spending two harrowing hours with several fritzing Road Homebots, they broke Jake and he hung up the phone and cried. Then I cried because Road Home made Jake cry. Finally, we both wiped our noses and went to rent a floor sander. But now we were considering retreat. We had met people who thought they might be eligible for assistance who had decided the wisest course of action was not to try. It seemed both ridiculous and sage.

Chris started up the front sidewalk. "Well, I'm going in," he shrugged, giving up. "See y'all downtown later?"

"Maybe," Jake said.

"They suck," I commented on the way home.

"Yeah," Jake replied. "And we suck. We need to stop working so much and get back on the house and finish it so we can start pretending this whole thing never happened."

"I know," I said.

"This stopped happening a year ago a few miles away," Jake said.

"I know," I said. "That's why I don't like to talk about it. Even if they're standing in it they don't see it still going on."

"We need to make it stop going on," Jake said.

"How?" I said. "Even if we're finished other people still won't be all around us. How can you finish when everyone can't get finished?"

"We just do," Jake said. "Pretend."

a bullet ant on the sting pain scale

Jake and I were riding in the back of his mom's car and his step-dad, Jack, was driving. It was late spring and Jake's birthday again and we were in Gainesville because Jake's stepmother and grand-mother had both just died. Rotten things had gotten only a little surprising. As Jack turned the corner, a thin old man grimaced and raised a leathery claw at the entrance to their subdivision.

"Oh no," I said. "Not you. Don't even look at us. I am not in the mood. Wave at yourself, dude."

"Is it him again? The dog nazi? You are kidding," Jake said. "No."

"Yes," I said, turning around in my seat to get another look. "Same guy. Only he lost his suspenders."

It was definitely the mean old Florida man from the evacua-tion almost three years before. The stand-up humanitarian who begrudged us refugees and our Nola mongrels a simple, poop-free jaunt around the block.

Jake gritted his teeth. Since his grandmother had suddenly slipped and fallen a few days after his stepmother died in hospice, his needle was in the red.

"*That* guy?" Jake said. "*He's* still here?"

I knew how he felt. A lot could evaporate in a few short years. Poof.

Jake's grandmother had helped raise Jake. She exclaimed *Good night!* when she was shocked like her mother probably had a hundred years before. When we were in town, she happily headed out to the local tattooed punks' hangout with us for dinner and talked politics and books she was reading. All of that and now, two weeks before her ninetieth party, the Atlanta girl was gone. Jake was crushed. He never got to deliver her fancy cake or the Mr. Han's Chinese special—chicken that supped exclusively on Jimmy Carter's peanuts.

Another perfectly lovely someone had slipped and fallen while mean old pick-up the-pee was probably still running dog walkers down, his ornery feet cold, gripping the ground. He would live to gripe another day. Oh, sometimes this world. Really.

"Alive and kicking," I said, squeezing Jake's hand. "Watch out."

"Whatever," Jake said.

"What? Who?" Brenda said.

"That's the guy who tried to make Cheryl pick up Clo's pee during the evacuation," Jake said. "That guy is why we can't walk Buster around your neighborhood anymore."

"Clo went in his yard?" Brenda said.

"That Clo was something," Jack said.

"No," Jake said. "She was just across the street in the little park. He's just anti-dog. A yeller."

Jack swung into their driveway. His hammock habitat restoration project in the middle of the well-manicured subdivision was getting green and rotten brown and forest dense. It was a tiny slice of bug and bird heaven. In spots, the bark mulch was so thick it was up to your knees. Half-sweet decay and dirt and peat perfumed the air. It was an abomination against all that was right and good and lawn Florida.

"Ah, we should walk Buster by anyway," Jack said. "Throw the old tennis ball in the park. Probably a bug hater. I've always thought a bug hater is a life hater."

* * *

Jack, Brenda, Buster, and I were strolling around Lake Alice one evening between funerals. Jake was off making sure his dad did not go crazy. He was taking his stepmother's minivan off his dad's hands and had swapped him the truck. Disaster truck would become beach truck. No more dump runs. Good-bye Clo and Buster on their hind legs, slobbering out either side of the truckbed on joyrides out of disasterville to City Park. Good-bye red cape and basset ears streaming in the wind. Now the truck would ferry his stepmother's orphaned labradoodle, Murray, around St. Augustine after his salty sunset swims.

By Lake Alice, it smelled like guano from the nearby bat house and community garden. Across the street, some Chinese families constructed bamboo and string trellises and gardened in a different language. College students sat on a bench near the tall bat house chewing potato chips. They were waiting for the sun to dip so they could get swooped.

"You sure you don't want to see the bats again?" Jack asked.

The beauty of flying bats I did not appreciate up close. They reminded me of the flying cockroaches in New Orleans.

"I can smell them from here," I said. "Maybe let's just walk until Buster wears out."

Jack blew his white bangs out of his eyes. He frowned at the lake. "I don't see any alligators today. The water's low. You know they moved some of the alligators? People were complaining."

"Did I ever tell you that the first time Jake's dad brought me to Florida he brought me out here? We fed marshmallows to the alligators," Brenda said.

"Oh, so it's your fault. That's why they come up to people," Jack said. "Thirty years of marshmallows will certainly do it."

"Yeah, ecocriminal," I said.

"Is it bad for them?" Brenda said.

"They looked fat and healthy," Jack said.

"You know the floods up north?" I said.

Jack nodded.

"It raised the Mississippi River so high they had to open the spillway to protect New Orleans. They hadn't done it in ten years. Last week they told people if you walk by certain parts of the Lakefront, watch out for alligators and snakes displaced from the spillway. Also dead flood cows."

"Geez," Jack said. "I bet everyone was thrilled about that with the levees and everything."

"No comment," I said. "But, yeah, some people were freaking. Nobody believes the Corps when they talk about safe heights and water pressure or pretty much anything anymore."

"I can imagine," Jack said.

Brenda shivered. "How can people live there worrying about stuff like that?"

I shrugged. "Hatchets in the attic. Denial. Canoes. Hope that somebody sensible is bound to come along and revamp the way they do things."

"Does Jake have an attic hatchet?" Brenda said.

"Yeah," I admitted. "He didn't before, but now he does. It's kind of old and flooded though."

"Good," she said. "That makes me feel better."

"But you have a second story," Jack said.

"Yep," I said. "This po-boy shop near our house? You should see it. They've got the little house next door raised up on this cement foundation and pilings to about twenty feet. Looks ridiculous. You know what they keep under it sometimes?"

Brenda shook her head.

"Motorboat," I said. "At first I thought it was for storage but now I don't know."

"That's one way," Jack said.

Brenda looked upset. "I just don't get the *reason* for all this," she said. "*Somebody* has to know what they're doing."

"You would think," I said.

Buster stopped short and rolled over onto his back into the grass at the edge of the water and began wiggling.

"Uh-oh. I think he found something terrible," Brenda said.

"Oh, that's a good stink. He's adding his stink to that stink and saying I'm alive," Jack said. "I have passed this way. Wait, is that an indigo bunting? I'll be darned!"

Brenda squinted. "Where?"

"Standing there in that mud patch in front of that grass."

We all stopped and squinted at this patch of tall grasses waving in the breeze near the edge of this mud island.

"See that blue? It looks like an indigo bunting," Brenda said.

"You know I think it is," Jack said. "I thought they had all flown off already. Shoot. I knew I should have brought my binoculars."

A jogger in a shiny tracksuit running on the path near us suddenly stopped in front of us. "The lake is not doing great. The lake is not doing nearly as well as it used to be," he said.

His affect was glassy, probably a little autistic. He pointed to a pile of brown sludge near the edge of the lake. It had a small turtle paddling desperately to keep his head above water near the edge of it.

"A part of that island in the middle broke off and floated to there," he said. "No one could stop it."

The jogger stood there glittering in that tracksuit. He seemed to be waiting for someone to speak.

"You know I was just telling her they had to move the alligators," Jack said.

The jogger just stared at him. Jack shifted uncomfortably. I bent down to pet Buster.

"Thank you for the information," Brenda finally said. And then the jogger sprinted off.

"Well, that was a little weird," Jack said. "How much more do you think old Buster has in him? I want to go on this trail."

"A little," I said. "It's not that hot."

"Don't get us in the chiggers," Brenda said.

Jack blushed. Once Jack had hiked Jake and I into some kind of vicious chigger's nest. It was worse than chicken pox. We were covered in cherry welts and took turns slapping each other for nearly a month.

"I still feel terrible about that," Jack said.

"We're over it," I said. "I promise. I absolve you. Go in peace."

"Maybe just don't do it again," Brenda said as we entered some trail near the edge of the lake thicket.

"What? This? There's a path," he said, pointing to a fifteen-inch strip of sand that cut through the trees and poison ivy. "Just stay on the path. Watch out for bullet ants!"

"That's not funny," Brenda said.

"Cheryl, did I tell you when I was in Costa Rica last month I got bit by a bullet ant? The old *Hormiga Veinticuatro*. A paraponera. I was very proud of myself. Those boogers are about this long," he said, holding an imaginary French fry between his thumb and forefinger.

"Is this going to turn into one of those fish stories about the one that got away?" I said.

"No, no," Jack said. "Well it *was* a big fish. But it didn't get away. It stung the hell out of me!"

"It was huge!" Brenda said. "I jumped on the bed."

"Sounds like a great trip," I said.

"There's this sting pain index for ranking the pain of different hymenoptera stings. A honey bee gets one rating, a paper wasp another. And bullet ant is the highest. A four plus! The *worst*. And I have now experienced the sting of the bullet ant."

Jack stopped on the path, turned around, and beamed. He was really proud of himself for getting stung by this bullet ant.

"It's really kind of a big deal, you know. In some areas of South America a boy can only become a man by being stung by a bullet ant," he said.

"Well," I said. "Did it hurt?"

"Oh, like the devil. It was terrible. And for a really, really long time."

Since his daughter had died, I often felt I should say something helpful or maybe buoyant to Jack, but I didn't quite know what. Instead I did the thing you're not supposed to do and rarely mentioned her. Jenny reminded me of Helen and I preferred not to think of all the little lights winging away.

"Oh," I said. "So if something really bad happens, you can say it was either like a honey bee or a bullet ant on the sting pain scale."

Jack laughed. "It's true," he said. "I guess you could."

"Well, congratulations. It's official. You can take a hit. And you lived to tell the tale."

"Yes I did," Jack said. "A four *plus*."

I thought of Jake. He'd been bit by the bullet ant, too, and didn't even know it meant anything but a big ouch. I reminded myself to tell him.

more about a neighborhood than you ever cared to know

Before the flood, we used to get a lot of guests in spring and fall. Either before or after the wet heat set in, that's when both expat New Orleanians and out-of-town friends tended to come looking for a sofa to crash. But once we got our living room back, the sofa stayed strangely empty.

The third spring after, though, something happened. The Chinese parasol shot up about five feet and waved hat-sized leaves on long bright green, bamboo-looking stalks near our front steps. Baby anoles bounded fence to hibiscus like cartoon lizards. My front and backyard looked like a regular New Orleans garden again—oversized, drooping, and decadent with blossoms. A monk parakeet sometimes left his squawking flock to sit alone on our transformer pole.

It wasn't the desperation garden it had been. It looked good. Better than your garden. Not the kind you needed to be a zealot or genius or millionaire to get, either. Just the garden everyone in New Orleans could have with enough time and soil. It looked like the kind of garden people who lived somewhere else might tear out of a magazine knowing they would never get the papaya and angel's trumpet and antique roses to bloom quite as plump.

And the phone started ringing. Friends who wanted to come visit and other friends trying to send us their friends called. We weren't ready yet.

"It must be on again," Jake remarked.

"Must be," I said. "People must consider it officially over. Now they all want their free place to stay back."

"I don't know if that's good or bad," Jake said.

"It's good," I said.

One nice thing about living in New Orleans has always been that if you are too busy or broke to go anywhere, a lot of the world still comes to you. Many people wanted to see New Orleans once. And friends who used to live here liked to come back and swing their legs off the edge of our porch and moan about how harried and boring and uptight and self-important life was where they were now. Yes, this was how all people spoke on vacation. But I had visited many of the places where these friends lived, so I believed them.

I had had a slight allergic reaction to some crawfish boil recently, but we were having an impromptu crawfish party. Some people said pop a Benadryl and eat them anyway but, considering I went so many perfectly happy vegetarian years between childhood and running back to the po-boy bosom, that seemed a little crazy. I was back to happily squeezing lemon on stuffed artichokes instead.

But Jake was a goner. He ate crawfish with the zealousness of a convert. All year long he was still mostly vegetarian but then come crawfish season he started downing ten pounds of crawfish tails and spice per week and washing it all down with strawberry beer. It was suicide.

One day, Jake got back from trying out some new crawfish stop. He was holding his stomach.

"I need to go lie down. Daryn and I had Big Al's. They're from Houma," he groaned. "Not as good as Zimmer's. Different from K-Jean's. But good."

"You know the reason you and Daryn feel sick is because nobody really eats that much crawfish a day," I said. "That's like pure city gluttony."

"What?" Jake said. "It's low-fat."

Tanio and Jeff were in town, and they were coming over for crawfish. I didn't really feel like giving The Tour. The Tour was starting to feel like going to confession. Forgive me, Father, for all I have done and all I have failed to do. Still, friends who had not been over for years, neighbors who had not been inside for weeks, curious strangers who had decided to rent a refurbished apartment in a once-flooded but now half-fixed neighborhood . . . it did not matter. Everyone expected the tour. My flood was their flood. They wanted to see how it was going. I was over it.

But I didn't mind giving Jeff the tour. He was my neuro-scientist-Sheetrocker. He had hung and floated with the best and worst of us. Jeff had put in a lot of long sweaty hours listening to old new wave music on satellite boombox with me. Before we hung the Sheetrock, he climbed the tall ladder and slid his long, skinny arms behind the wood strips of lathe traversing the studs while I stuffed fiberglass bats from below and coughed. He had gone from sweating and eating spicy turkey necks out of a bag for months to a post-doc at Harvard. I liked to pretend that I played an important role. I liked to listen to science public radio and quiz Jeff down so he would not get out of practice during his Sheetrock residency.

"I haven't seen it all painted," Jeff said. "Looks great."

We were in the living room. We had new bicycles and new ceiling fans and a bright yellow painting of a Mardi Gras Indian chief who had died of a heart attack addressing the New Orleans City Council about the NOPD. Jake gave me the painting for Christmas. The artist used to be an auto body painter. Since the painting was a copy, he said he had put a few extra twinkles in Tootie Montana's braids and eyes. I really liked it. I hoped it didn't make me the worst kind of New Orleans hippie.

"Well, it's not all painted, but down here is. Actually it might be the exact same light blue your parents have. Weird. Presenting the office," I said, dragging open the pocket doors. "Such that it is."

What was supposed to be my office was where the paint cans and drills and table saw and stripped molding and t-square sat in piles. We needed to haul everything to the attic and sand the floor and paint the walls. I pointed to this almost perfect table.

"Dave and Jake just made that," I said.

"That's really impressive," Jeff said.

"Yeah. I know. Who knew? But I think Jake did the grunt part. Still learning. Dave's like this master carpenter now. You should see this molding he did. He has all these routers and attachments. He can do curves."

Dave was disappointed Jake had gotten rid of the truck. He wanted to know who was going to drive us all to the dump now. But a few times in the past few months, I had come home and caught Jake sitting in the stairwell practicing his bass and humming. I was shocked by how long it had been. He had mostly ignored calls from music people for a long time and had only played with a few guys since the flood. It felt like we were finally maybe just beginning to get back to normalish. If Dave wanted us to haul him to the dump in a truck for the rest of our lives, tough!

"The doors look great," Jeff said.

"Stripease guy puts them in chemicals but that makes them furry. I have about ten to sand," I said. "I'm not taking you upstairs. Some of it's better; some is not. I lost steam. This house is too big. We'll never finish it."

"You will," Jeff said. "It may take you a decade."

"Don't even say that," I said.

Since the late eighties, Jeff's family had been restoring an old New Orleans mansion in the Lower Garden District with some kind of cistern or moat underneath. It was beautiful. His father had sent me a rare fern from a California spore. Our house wasn't half that size, but Jeff's much larger family worked on his. Flood or no flood, someone in New Orleans was always battling old properties.

"It looks a lot better than it looked last August. A lot. You had half of what's finished finished when I was here last," Jeff said.

"Okay. My goal then is not to ruin my life and also finish it before you come back again."

Tanio could no longer come for a visit without us winding up with another machine. A guy on the West Bank of New Orleans sold amusement machine parts and recycled stale Mardi Gras Moon Pies as package stuffing. When Tanio came to visit, he had a box of Moon Pies and capacitors waiting for him. In the unfinished side of the house, I still had the refurbished Toobin'. This year Tanio and Jake had found a fifty-dollar Aladdin's Castle harem pinball machine. When Tanio got to town, he had gotten out his dad's pity card table and put on my straw hat and sat by the strawberry bottlebrush tree and soldered in the sun. Now he sat on Helen's backyard glider spooning potato salad into his mouth.

"Did you see that Moog documentary?" Jeff said.

"Nope," Tanio said.

"With the Rick Wakeman guy from Yes?" Jake said.

"Yup," Jeff smiled.

Jake started laughing.

"Man I have to see that," Tanio said.

Buster disappeared into the plants. When Clo was still around, she dug a cool spot between some irises and a Lakeview jasmine. It was Buster's cool spot now. I could see his dark eyes glinting between the slender green stalks.

"You playing any?" Jeff asked.

"A few times," Jake said. "Guess it feels like the good part might turn into the same ten years of work I might be dumb to do again."

"I've been going up to Tanglewood a lot," Jeff said.

"You're the only one there under seventy," I ventured.

"That's not true," Jeff said. "Well, kind of. At first."

The dollhouse kitchen looming over our backyard was finally closed and painted a pale yellow. Some nights when the moon hit it the right way, the branches of a tree in a nearby abandoned backyard shook and danced across it in gargantuan silhouette. Helen's moonwalking monster was now an enormous shadow puppet. From another abandoned yard, a wild patch of banana fronds waved.

A bright orange house door served for our garden gate. Dave and Marcelle pushed a stroller through. Buster trotted out of the irises and stuck his nose on the stroller, gingerly sniffing this new baby's feet.

"What's the baby's name?" Tanio said.

"Lily," Dave said. "We named the baby after our dog. Maybe I should stop saying that."

"Getting any sleep yet?" I asked. "Your families still here?"

"My stepfather came to visit," Dave said. "He hated our neighborhood. He's this Marine state cop guy; he just got back from Fallujah and he kept asking me for a gun. He kept saying I'd feel a lot better if I had a gun to walk around here."

"Maybe you just shouldn't walk around at night a lot," Jake suggested.

"It was all the time!" Dave said.

"Maybe you should just have given him yours to shut him up," I said.

"She made me get rid of it!" Dave said, thumbing toward Marcelle.

Marcelle gave Dave a look. She pushed her glasses up her nose and nodded toward the tiny baby.

"It's cool," Dave said. "I got a PlayStation 3 instead."

I glanced at Jake. In a way, Dave had infected Jake with his gun madness and now his gun was gone and ours wasn't. What the hell? Jake shrugged.

"Is that the system you were playing the other day? The game textures look a lot better than they used to. The gravel looks like gravel. The wood looks like wood," I said.

Dave glanced up from the crawfish card table. He was standing and cleaning shells and eating.

"Was I an assassin or a hit man?" he said, popping a crawfish tail into his mouth.

"I don't know," I said. "Old buildings. Looked like the Middle East."

"Assassin's Creed," he said.

"Normal mapping," Tanio said.

"Whatever it is, it's awesome," Dave said.

I gave Marcelle the garden tour. The slab where the shed had been was now lined with big planters. I had Meyer lemon and key lime trees. The Confederate jasmine's star blossoms fizzed white, coating the trellis in sugar and dark leaves.

"There's the blueberry you gave me," I said.

Marcelle pointed to the pomegranate tree. "Was that here last time? It's huge."

"Isn't that crazy?" I said. "From just last year. It just got big all of a sudden. We netted it because of the birds. The other day Buster got twisted like a fish in the net."

Marcelle touched a leaf of the small lemon tree. "I got one of those, too. My lemons flowered and flowered but never gave any fruit," she said.

"Huh," I said. "Hope that doesn't happen to me."

It was weird fixing your house at the same time as ten other people you knew were fixing theirs. Dave, and Marcelle and Jake and I had all decided on the same sink and it got on all our nerves in the same way. Dave and Marcelle still had a few odds and ends to do, but they were mostly finished. House fixing wasn't a race, but if it was, survival Dave had won and we had lost. He had gotten ahead and even come to help us hang some trim to try to catch up.

Was it because their house was smaller? Because one of them was a bigger slave driver? Because they had more energy? Because they hired more help? Because no one they knew died or got shot? Because we sucked? A few times I had gotten angry after going over there and seeing some new Mexican tile or something and vowed, Dave and Marcelle are not going to finish before we do! I can't stand it! Sometimes I preferred to walk by some of our still-working friends on other blocks.

"I haven't been upstairs in a while," Marcelle said. "Dave said you finished your bedroom."

"Yeah. It's great. Sometimes it's hard to appreciate the finished stuff because I'm seeing all that's left to do," I said. "I think if we both took six to eight weeks off and had a little help we could vanquish it once and for all. I hate the idea of weekend and nighting it for another year."

"Yeah," Marcelle said, lifting the baby from the stroller. "There's that two months off of work part. Let's see it."

Lily was tiny. She was embarking on her first flooded house tour. Hopefully by the time she was old enough to remember, there would be no more flooded house renovation tours.

If I started a reality show and had to pick a team for *Flood Survivor*, I'd have spots for all the ladder ladies still painting and fixing houses across town. I'd have a spot for the old man next door who was singing an old spiritual under my window, "I'm Going Home," scraping paint from his family's house on the other side of the barbed wire. And I'd definitely have two spots for Dave and Marcelle.

Marcelle was chased by a drunk and screaming flood worker waving a bottle and had to bolt through the flood zone. She went to court over the chasing, sweated and hammered on two-story scaffolding nailing up siding, worked full-time, and had a baby. Dave had painted and hammered and sawed and nailed and sanded to fix his house. He had helped fix and reopen and run one flooded and two other restaurants and played in a few bands. No one I knew who lived outside the flood zone here or in other cities and liked to whine about how stressful their jobs and lives were had done anything close.

When they left later, Dave had a plastic bag of crawfish tails. "Y'all come to Ray's Boom Boom for the show," he said.

Something happened to Dave's Rush cover band and now he was in a Latin funk band that kind of did Spanish versions of old New Orleans soul hits. Or something like that. They were pretty good. I only heard Tom Sawyer now when Dave's cell phone rang.

Jake passed a big bowl of leftover crawfish across the fence to Pastor Jim, the same fence Pastor Jim had hung over to point a gun at the shed thief.

"Should I send the potato salad, too?" Jake called.

"Whatever," I said.

"Y'all are going to fatten me up," Pastor Jim said from the other side of the fence.

After everyone left, Tanio helped me bag the garbage.

"I don't know why, but people seem less stooped this year. If you had told me that first trip that it would get back to half normal, I wouldn't have believed you," Tanio said. "Even last summer I wouldn't have believed it."

"I did tell you that I thought that. Or hoped it. You were like *run for your lives!*"

"Was I? Jeez. Well, I was wrong. Maybe," Tanio said. "I just notice people are just walking around different. Happier."

"Everybody got used to it. We got electricity. Or maybe you just don't see some of the people I do. I'll take you to the coffee shop and introduce you to this roofer friend I know who used to be a cop, who's living in this formaldehyde trailer with cancer," I said. "They want to take his trailer but he isn't finished his house yet. It's a mess."

Tanio winced. "Please don't. Let me just stick with my first glance assessment if you don't mind," he said. "Did I tell you Dad said he got some drifters to help him fix some stuff?"

"No," I said. "He better watch it with that."

"You wouldn't believe the labor trouble he's had," he said.

"I would," I said.

A local businesman had recently come pounding on a neighbor's door looking for the contractor who had robbed him of $8,000. Jake assured him no contractor lived there. The man looked ready to beat someone's ass. He left disappointed. Some other contractor had also sponsored a cruel "Why My Family Deserves a New House" essay contest for flooded New Orleans children.

As soon as Tanio plopped on the sofa next to Jake, Buster stood up and started barking. And barking. Deep, loud, and heinous.

"Please shut up," I said.

"What's wrong with him?" Tanio said.

Everyone knew Buster didn't bark much. Buster was the lounging type. Clo had been our barker.

"He wants his Clo treat," Jake said. "It got late and we forgot. He does that every night at eight now."

"What?" Tanio said.

"His commemorative Clo treat," I said. "She barked at eight for their treat. After she was gone, he started. He's tossing one back for his departed."

Tanio smiled. "Ah, so what I'm hearing is Clo taught him the bad habit of demanding a treat at a certain time every night and you caved," he said.

"Basically, yes," I said.

"That's sweet," Tanio said.

Jake got up and pulled a green dental bone off the mantel. "Here," he said. "Want to do the honors?"

"Yes," Tanio said.

Recently, a musician Jake knew had come to town from Brazil. The night we saw him on Frenchmen Street he sat in with a big avant-jazz group. A lot of the baby anarchists I call Oliver Twisters were there. Avant-jazz is one of my least favorite forms of entertainment, but I liked checking out the Twisters' fingerless gloves and knee pants and battered tweed poverty stylings. Ceiling fans were spinning. People were grinning and hanging over the balcony. I liked leaning over to Jake and whispering, "Give me my gruel. Give me my figgy pudding."

Any new bouncing baby anarchists of Southern or whatever persuasion had a place to call home. There they were on Frenchmen and there they should be. Near the ex-Goths, near the left-behind crusty punks, near the trustafarians, drug addicts, musicians, cruisers, tourists, hat wearers, nighttime strollers, and off-duty strippers.

Oliver Twisters you could count on. But whenever I was trying my best to trust the Corps again, they would flake out on me. This summer they had been busted using newspaper filling instead of rubber for some floodwall fixes. They were like the one-eyed roofer Pastor Jim had recommended to re-roof our own botched roofing over our small back roof. One-eyed Roofer had overcharged us and torched down leaky scraps from another job. When it rained, water streamed into our newly Sheetrocked kitchen and dining room. Jake and I fixed One-Eyed Roofer's fix ourselves three times before giving up, searching for another roofer, and paying for it all again. Then we repainted our walls and ceilings. We would never finish if we wasted all our time re-fixing fixes. Neither would the Corps.

The basic levee and floodwall maintenance and design problems revealed by the flood remained shocking. Recently water had been seeping through the 17th Street Canal that had flooded our house. The Corps had finally agreed to an independent assessment of the puddling. Would it be Californians or Europeans? No one knew.

I hoped some Dutch Satchmo would get here with his clipboard quick. I doubted any 9-11 widow would offer us a place in the happy cheese town again. Why should she? Now there were Burmese cyclone people and Chinese earthquake people, Iowa flood people, and more. Since the Oakland Hills fire ladies brought their emergency information packets to us, California wildfires had freshly sooted many new faces. Tomorrow's disaster people were skipping and licking a lollipop with their own landslide just up the hill.

One tired morning after a night spent sweating in our bed and vowing not to throw any more money at air-conditioning or our house because of worry about the future of New Orleans, Jake got irritated that I was wiffle-waffling after all we had been through. "You can't live your life with one foot out the door," he said.

"I'm not," I said. But I was lying. Some days I felt brave; other days I just felt scared.

I rarely went to neighborhood association meetings anymore. Sometimes I was even behind on my cheap dues. Mostly I just followed our e-mail list.

The detailed blow-by-blow of human nature from our corner of the city was not exactly uplifting. E-mail blasts detailed sagas like which poor people stole which richer mom's custom stroller and the manhunt to retrieve it. Apparently a number of New Orleanians found cause to stab someone with a kitchen knife. Other blasts featured the bicycling dog thief, pro- and anti-convenience store crusaders, and the crack flophouse that had been leaning but had just blazed to a crisp. People planned to turn old funeral homes and cemeteries into haunted houses and ghost-hunting laboratories near other people's just-fixed houses and those people hated them. Bloggers got pistol-whipped and wanted to social-network it out. Other e-mail blasters demanded to know what was in that stink water they finally pumped out of the flooded hospital or longed simply to be left alone. Some days it was really more about a neighborhood than you ever cared to know.

But I volunteered to do the gutted/not-gutted survey again. For some reason the city could not accomplish this alone, so the neighborhood associations got involved. I had completed the surveys several times since the flood. From talking to people on dog walks, I knew what in my area was really gutted, fake gutted, and what had never been touched at all. I had chatted with returning line cooks who were petrified the leaning house next door would fall on their house. I had picked through five-foot weeds to peek into moldy and tossed living rooms, saying hola! to flood workers and how are y'all? to skinny young drug dealers.

I wasn't looking forward to surveying again. I wanted this to be my last. Peeking in abandoned windows with my pen and checklist made me feel like a professional busybody. Since the last survey, a few perfectly salvageable historic houses had been hosed down, chewed up by yellow cranes, and scooped into dump trucks. Other houses that were caving in on themselves still stood. The second dollhouse on my block—the one on the corner, not the one in my backyard, had recently been demolished. Some neighbors had snuck in and tried to salvage woodwork before the cranes came, but some other neighbors had called the cops on them.

A few months before, Mrs. Dupre, my neighbor across the street with the Virgin Mary grotto, came with her bearded grandson and a moving truck to pick up a few last pieces of flooded furniture. Mr. Dupre had died since we last saw him sitting white as a ghost in the backseat of a car in front of their flooded house.

"I came to get my Mary. She's the last thing. I've been looking for you," Mrs. Dupre said, slipping something into my shirt pocket. "That's for you and for your husband watching my place so good. For you taking care of my Mary."

I had been pulling potato chip bags and construction trash out of her grotto and pulling weeds and keeping construction fliers off the door so no one would know their house was abandoned. The irises I had replanted in her grotto had bloomed again this year. But pit bull Jesus and the hurricane miracle seemed so long ago. And the days when her husband was smiling in his golf cap and suspenders before the flood seemed like a dream. I felt funny about taking her money, but I knew better than to refuse.

"I've been happy to do it. Now Jake will want me to take him out to lunch," I joked.

"That's going to be some kind of lunch," she said, leaning in to whisper. "A hundred dollars. Get that somewhere safe inside."

"We really appreciate it," I told her. "Thank you."

"No. I'm paying for all this work. We finally sold it to Road Home. I hated to but nobody would give me a fair price," she said. "I'm never coming back again. After I leave here today, my life is over. That's it."

"No, it's not," I protested. "It's changing."

"No. This life is over," she said. She reached out her arms and gave me a hug.

"I took care of my mother for years on Tulane Avenue. Was glad to do it. Now my mother's gone. My husband's gone. We raised our kids. We had a life. Then we went to bingo and the church senior center every day. All gone. Now what am I supposed to do?"

Her bearded grandson and his friend hoisted Mary from her grotto. Mrs. Dupre looked dubious. "Be careful with that!" she called.

"Why can't we just say that your new life is beginning?" I said.

It sounded like one of the stupid things younger people say to whitewash older people's pain. But it was all I had. Mrs. Dupre rolled her eyes.

"I'm here to say good-bye," she told me. "But maybe. We'll see."

Now it was ninety degrees in the morning and the top of my head started frying. Time for the survey. The armed rapist in his white undershirt and the old man who dealt drugs years before the storm but didn't seem to now were sitting on a front porch a block away. The Sewerage and Water Board truck had busted up our street for the umpteenth time. The smell of hot, raw sewerage soiled the air.

There was a new breakfast place on a corner where a liquor store used to be and old houses with new paint jobs and flagpoles that looked better than they had in a decade. There was no space for that on the form. The spaces were for the other things.

Back door not secured for over six months. Litter. Waist high grass, leaning, rats, vines growing through upstairs window. Not gutted, not secured, pre storm blight, has had same junk on porch for years. FEMA trailer leaking sewerage onto sidewalk. These are the types of things I was supposed to write on the forms every year until there was nothing left to write.

What would happen to many of these left-behind houses was unclear. Sometimes when I was working in my front garden, old neighbors drove by, rolled down a window, and called out things like, "Hey, baby, we're stuck on the West Bank now."

This blazing hot summer survey morning, people said other things.

Can someone please ask the church not to rent that building out for a day labor center again? My son just bought this property next to it. How can he possibly make it nice with old jalopies and groups of men coming and going? It was never zoned for that. Who can I call? That guy who bought all these properties and is renting them Section Eight? He has so many extra people in them. Parole officers keep coming by. Who can I call? This man on the corner? His house is so raised he didn't flood and still he has not cut that high grass or picked up trash in two years! Who can I call? This contractor left this pile of construction trash and tires here for the last six months. Who can I call? This house is about to fall on us. Who can I call? By the time you finished hearing people's problems, you wished you were a professional busybody or the mayor or the governor or a city inspector or anyone who could and would actually do something.

Was I going to tell someone? Was I going to remind them? Was I going to write it down? Yes, I said. Yes and yes and yes. Hopefully it would help.

acknowledgments

Thanks to Amy Pyle, Michaela Hamilton, Karen Auerbach, Susan Higgins, and everyone at Kensington Citadel. Special thanks to Levine Greenberg Literary Agency, especially Lindsay Edgecombe and Daniel Greenberg, for patience through one disastered novel, some rebuilding, and a few years. Much appreciation also to Pete Jordan, Doug Gruse, Paul Tough, Julie Snyder, Ira Glass, Alex Blumberg, Lisa Pollak, Jim Whorton, Peter Cooley, Jack Pendarvis, Anne Choi, Craig Taylor, Jonathan Goldstein, Dedra Johnson and Rick Barthelme.

More thanks to Dave Greengold, Marcelle Rousseau, Paul Gailiunas, Becky Lewis, Courtney Egan, David Sullivan, Jeff Wingard, Denise Michelet, Ken Rayes, Tim Watson, Brad Richard, Alice Kennedy, Brad Clark, Sam Clark, Alex Hemard, Bobbie Jones, Stoo Odom, Lou C., Stan H., Stan W., Aaron Brindle, Jason Fontenot, Kevin Walters, Daryn DeLuco, and Brian Madden. Thank you Tim S., Adam L., Adam K., Ron C., and others for getting filthy with us. Gratitude to James Pepersack, Keith, Steve, Melinda, Casey C., Martin H., and everyone who gave construction advice, shared a Popsicle, or loaned us a tool. Thanks to Tanio Klyce for soldering and batch files. Chris Kirsch and Andrew Lee provided scooter-based comic relief. Thanks to Elizabeth W., Jack S., Brenda S., and Jim S. for everything and the New Orleans JCC for letting disaster people shower for cheap. Special thanks to all our do-it-yourself neighbor friends. Thank you, Deanna and

Dempsey S., all S's, Billy Crews, Jim Findley, Jamie Ramoneda, Dotty Klyce, Katrina Marino, Victoria Klyce, and Steve Klyce. Appreciation to Anthony DelRosario, Craig Roberts, Sarah Prior, Gene Gutenberg, and anyone whose kindness I have mercifully forgotten. Biggest, bestest thanks to Jake—let's never tell this particular story again.